About the Author

Mary Fane-Gladwin was born in 1957 and went to school at
St. Mary's, Ascot. She went on to study fine art at Falmouth Art
School and has since worked in advertising and design.

She now lives in Windsor, Berkshire.

Channel Island Hopping

A Handbook for the Independent Traveller

MARY FANE-GLADWIN

SPHERE BOOKS LIMITED
30–32 Gray's Inn Road, London WC1X 8JL

First published in Great Britain by Sphere Books Ltd,
in association with Gentry Books Ltd, 1982
Copyright © Mary Fane-Gladwin

Printed in Finland by Werner Söderström Oy,
a member of Finnprint

Contents

Introduction *11*

Island Government *16*

Part I   **Jersey** *23*
The Island Today *24*
A Short History *29*
How to get to the Island *45*
Inter-Island Travel *50*
Travel within the Island *53*
Where to Stay *60*
Eating and Entertainment *70*
Leisure Activities *76*

Part II   **Guernsey** *99*
The Island Today *101*
A Short History *106*
How to get to the Island *117*
Inter-Island Travel *121*

Travel within the Island   *124*
Where to Stay   *129*
Eating and Entertainment   *139*
Leisure Activities   *141*

Part III   **Alderney**   *167*
The Island Today   *168*
A Short History   *171*
How to get to the Island   *180*
Inter-Island Travel   *182*
Travel within the Island   *183*
Where to Stay   *187*
Eating and Entertainment   *193*
Leisure Activities   *197*

Part IV   **Sark**   *205*
The Island Today   *207*
A Short History   *210*
How to get to the Island   *219*
Travel within the Island   *220*
Where to Stay   *222*
Eating and Entertainment   *224*
Leisure Activities   *225*

Part V   Herm *231*
        The Island Today *233*
        A Short History *236*
        How to get to the Island *240*
        Where to Stay *241*
        Leisure Activities *243*
        Eating and Entertainment *244*
        What to See *245*

Part VI   Miscellanea *247*
        Uninhabited Islands *248*
        Flora and Fauna *252*
        Channel Island Calendar *257*
        Customs *261*

Bibliography *267*

List of Maps

The Channel Islands 15
Jersey: The Island Today 22
St Helier: The Town Centre 26
Jersey: The Beaches 78
Jersey: What to See 93
Guernsey: The Island Today 103
St Peter Port 129
Guernsey: The Beaches 143
Guernsey: What to See 157
Alderney: The Beaches 196
Alderney: What to See 166
Sark: What to See 206
Sark: The Beaches 230
Herm: 232

This book is dedicated to my grandmother, Daisy Prescott-Westcar

Particular thanks go to:

My Father and Denise

Jackie Houghton

Christopher Burness and Paula Levey

Mr Salmon and the Guernsey Tourist Board

Major and Mrs Peter Wood

Dr and Mrs Murfitt

Catriona and Clare Murfitt

Mrs Worthsley and Jane Worthsley

Mrs Guilliard

Mr and Mrs L'Apelle and National Trust
  for Guernsey

Mrs Carey

Mrs Dickson and The Societe Jersiaise

Victor Coyshe

Carol Toms

Anne Simeon

And last but not least thanks go to all the
rest of my family, and friends for their help and support.

Introduction

On a globe of the world you cannot see them at all. On a map of Europe they are hardly discernable. On a navigational chart of the English Channel they are apparent, but have no great significance. Yet these tiny bits of land have an influence which is out of all proportion to their size.

Who in the western world does not wear a jersey? Who in Britain is not familiar with the creamy yellow contents of the gold top bottles on their doorsteps, or the perfect round red fruit in cartons on the market stalls? Ask anybody the name of an American state and they will almost certainly say New York. Ask any New Yorker the same question and the odds are that he will say New Jersey. He may even add that his favourite holiday play-ground is known locally as the Jersey Shore. Perhaps he is descended from one of the original 300 islanders selected from the islands to settle in the New World.

Jersey might even have an earlier connection with America. The Irish monk St Brendan is now believed by many to have beaten Columbus to it by about 900 years. It is said that St Brendan built a chapel in Jersey, where St Brelades Church now stands, when he was blown off course by a storm in his search for the blessed land in the

West. America's blessings are returned in the warm Gulf Stream waves lapping the island beaches, which last licked land on a Caribbean shore and give the south coast of Jersey a character more in keeping with the Mediterranean than the Atlantic. These islands have been inhabited since Paleaolithic times, and formed part of Gaul during the time of the Roman Empire. The Romans did not appreciate the value to be had from living there themselves. Instead they exploited those who did by extracting taxes.

According to local lore, the Channel Islanders were recruited to sail with a Duke, of Norse descent, to conquer England in 1066. It may have been the arrow of an islander which pierced the eye of the Saxon king, putting King William I on the throne of England and a touch of Island blood into the veins of some of us. For a century and a half afterwards the descendants of King William ruled on both sides of the English Channel. Then one unlucky scion lost his treasure in the wash, most of his feudal powers at Runnymede and all of Normandy, except the Channel Islands. But King John must have had some good points for the Channel Islanders to remain loyal to him!

In the centuries that followed, fort-building became a thriving industry and fending off the French a major preoccupation. Wars came and went and at one time during the Napoleonic era the island of Sark was over-run by 400 Frenchmen, but eventually they grew tired of waiting and just went home. Perhaps nobody told them that as far as Sark is concerned, advanced booking is a *must*.

By 1940 Britain had decided that the islands were indefensible and let the Germans walk in. The moribund fortification building industry was again revived but few islanders benefitted from this rennaissance. The work was mainly undertaken by East Europeans imported specially for the task, but whose terms of contract were decidedly unattractive. The islanders have never shunned hard work, but let's admit it, everybody prefers to be paid first rate for the job.

Throughout their history the islanders have excelled in any occupation they liked doing best, and have successfully made it work for them. Beggars can not be choosers, so when the demand for knitted goods became overwhelming the island men, pressganged by the ladies, knitted. They must have made a good team, because Mary Queen of Scots is said to have been beheaded still wearing a pair of Guernsey knitted stockings.

Privateering was a job which they seemed to like doing best. Licensed piracy against their foes on the high seas made many an islander prosperous from the spoils of war. Continental visitors will be pleased to hear that this is no longer practised, even on the Condor Hydrofoil! Later, when piracy was no longer considered original, fortunes were made a little more peaceably. Many of the large manor houses in Jersey date from a time when the Islanders sailed to the Newfoundland Banks and fished for cod. Banks yielding even better returns for islanders today are named, National Westminster, Barclays, Lloyds and a host of others as witnessed by the rows of brass plates lining the streets of St Helier. If the islands are still under threat of invasion today, it is most likely to be from Zurich, or even Bermuda.

Less adventurous ways of making money were found in the use of natural materials. For years the miles of island coastline were scoured for seaweed, known locally as 'Vraic', pronounced 'rack'. Dried and burnt, the ashes made the best natural form of fertiliser.

One tradition which has not yet been superceded by the 20th century is the 'Clameur de Haro', which is unique to the islands. If you think someone is doing harm to your property, grab a witness and in the presence of this witness pronounce the 'Clameur de Haro' and everyone will have to stop what they are doing until the mess is sorted out in court.

Finally, do not worry about any language problem when you come to the Channel Islands. Today, most of the French you will hear spoken is by a Continental day-tripper who thinks nothing of spending the day on a shopping spree, which usually ends up in Marks and Spencers. You will probably spend the evening drinking with new found friends in the island pubs which are most famous for their relaxed licensing laws and cheap alcohol. So when you arrive, forget all your worries it is easy to enjoy oneself in the Channel Islands.

ENGLAND

☆ Southampton

Weymouth
☆

Isle of Wight

N

ENGLISH CHANNEL

CASQETS ⋮ ALDERNEY

☆ Cherbourg

GUERNSEY ● HERM
● SARK

PATERNOSTER ●.
● ECRÉHOUS

JERSEY

THE CHANNEL
ISLANDS ●.

MINQUIERS

FRANCE

☆ Granville

☆
St Malo

0   20 miles

Island Government

A Short History

The Channel Islands have an unusual system of Government within the British Isles. They are run autonomously and are very proud of their independence which can be traced back to the time of William the Conqueror. Any islander today will tell you that his loyalty lies with the Queen, even though the Channel Islands are independent territories of the crown and do not form part of the United Kingdom. To explain this anomaly, some reference must be drawn to events leading up to the present day.

At the time of the Norman conquest, Duke William divided the islands and incorporated his 'Fief du Roi' into the newly acquired Norman Anglo State. He gave some land to religious houses, and other property to friends who built manor houses and exercised their Seigneurial rights. Until that time all the islands had been run along feudal lines with courts presided over by a judiciary and his 'Jurats' (judges chosen from among the islanders) to give sentence on any cases, which were heard. As time progressed a Lord of the Islands was appointed by the English

Crown to keep the individual islands in check. It was an honorary title, and few Lords took any interest in these small pieces of land. King John was no exception and it was only when he lost Normandy in 1202 that he realised their strategic position. They were the last remaining territories left between England and Normandy, he went to to great lengths to ensure that the islanders remained loyal to him. In return he granted them a charter in which he outlined their rights and promised to defend them against their enemies.

Succeeding Lords of the Islands had a more difficut task since England was at war with France and the islands were vulnerable and in urgent need of defence. So that they could carry out their duty a Warden was appointed who was nearly always an expert in military procedure or an ex-soldier who could act on behalf of the lord. As the Wardens spent a greater period of time making military decisions it was soon clear that without somebody responsible for the civil administration on the islands they would soon be in even greater chaos. Hence the position of Bailiff was created. At first he was chosen by the Warden, but later as his duties grew it became important that the office was held by an islander. Difficulties lay not only with the practical problems of keeping the islands under English rule at such a distance but also because the islands were all operating under a different Norman/French language. Inevitably problems arose within the administration of the islands, and during the reign of Henry VII they were divided into two 'Bailiwicks'. Jersey on the one hand, and Guernsey, Alderney and Sark on the other. At this point the major island decisions were handled by the Privy Council in London who rose to the occasion when islanders presented petitions, or made complaints against their Bailiff which has occurred frequently throughout their history. Today the administration on the islands has changed to accommodate the needs of the twentieth century but they are one of the oldest forms of government in the world with a unique constitution.

How the islands are run today

The Channel Islands have their own legislative assemblies and legal administrative systems. Their laws depend on their validity on the orders made by the Queen in Council. HM Government is responsible for the defence and international relations of the islands and the Crown is ultimately responsible for their good government.

The Islands are divided into 2 Bailiwicks: Jersey is one, Guernsey, Alderney, Herm and Sark is the other. The Sovereign representative in each Bailiwick is the Lieutenant Governor who is the official channel of communication between HM Government in the United Kingdom and the islands. Jersey and Guernsey each have a Bailiff, also appointed by the Crown.

In **Jersey** the island government is known as the Assembly of the States comprising 12 Senators (elected by popular franchise every 6 years, six retiring every third year), 12 constables, one for each parish (elected every 3 years) and 29 deputies (elected by popular franchise throughout the parishes). The Dean of Jersey, the Attorney General and the Solicitor General are also entitled to sit in the States although they have no vote.

The Royal Court consists of the Bailiff and 12 jurats who are elected to office by an Electoral College. The Court sits in two ways, either as a Full Court known as Le Nombre Supériur which consists of the Bailiff, Deputy Bailiff and 7 jurats for more serious cases, or as Le

Nombre Inferieur which requires less members: the Bailiff and Deputy Bailiff and only 2 jurats, for routine civil or criminal business. The States of Jersey also have separate committees for each Field of Public Business such as Education or Tourism, and each of these is headed by a President.

In order to vote in Jersey you must be over 18 years of age and conform to residential qualifications which vary according to each parish. Providing you have been resident on the island since the 1st of March of any one year and are a British citizen or from the Repubic of Ireland you are entitled to vote that same year.

Jersey is well known as a tax haven. There is no VAT here, or Capital Gains Tax. However, in order to protect the residents on the island certain protective measures have been introduced over the last decade. Unless already a resident, or someone who the States consider as an 'essential employee' such as a teacher or doctor, you must have lived on the island for 10 years before becoming a resident which enables the buying of any property. Another exception to the rule are wealthy immigrants who are allowed to live on the island and enjoy the benefits of this tax haven providing they can fulfill certain qualifications. This was formerly gauged by monetary status. The number of permitted entries has dropped considerably in recent years to an average of 15 or less each year, and immigrants' applications are judged according to their capacity to contribute to the Islands' economy.

In **Guernsey** the Bailiff presides over the representative Assembly known as The States and the Royal Court.

This constitutes an island parliament and is divided into two sections with combined responsibility for legislature. The legislature bodies are divided as follows: The States of Deliberation, which consists of the Bailiff; 12 'conseill-

eurs', who are elected by the 'electoral college'; 33
Deputies who are elected by public franchise; and 10
Douzeniers elected by the parish council. Proceedings are
conducted in English and any member of the public may be
admitted to the Court House in St Peter Port to listen to
the deliberations.

The States of Election which consists of the Bailiff; 33
sitting members of the States of Deliberation (deputies); 12
jurats of the Royal Court; and 34 Douzeniers. The
Douzeniers are elected by the parishes, of which there are
10 in Guernsey. The Deputies are elected by the people of
Guernsey. Elections are held every 3 years in March and
providing that you are aged over 20 and have been resident
on the island from the 1st day of October from the
preceding electoral year you are entitled to vote.

Civil and criminal cases are heard in the Royal Court
which is the oldest form of Island Government and consists
of the Bailiff and 12 jurats, or sworn judges. The Court is
open to the public when it is in session and, although
proceedings are conducted in English, certain traditional
deliberations are read in French.

The Courts of **Alderney** and **Sark** have limited power
and deal with legislative and petty criminal offences on the
island. In **Alderney** the States consists of the President
who is elected to this life-long post by popular vote, and 12
elected state members who are voted for by the island
electorate. The Alderney Court is headed by a Chairman
and 3 or more jurats – it always must be an uneven
number. Both posts are appointed by the Home Office and
this court has the power to impose fines of up to £100 and
2 months imprisonment. Major criminal cases are heard in
Guernsey where there is an island prison which can hold
offenders for a maximum 3-year sentence. Prisoners
receiving longer sentences are transferred to a State prison

on the mainland.

In **Sark** the island parliament is known as the Chief Pleas and 12 deputies are elected by public franchise. The Sénéschal's Court is the sole Court of Justice on the island and hears only minor criminal offences. Any major cases are dealt with by the Royal Court in Guernsey, although this is a rare occurrance. The Island of Herm forms part of St Peter Port Parish and comes under the jurisdiction of Guernsey.

The residential qualifications in Guernsey are extremely complicated and although newcomers are entitled to buy any house on the island that is on the open market (as opposed to the substantially cheaper local market houses) there is no guarantee that he will actually be able to occupy it. Open market houses are generally in the region of £100,000 upwards. In order to live on the island a licence must be obtained from the States and in order to obtain this the applicant must fulfill certain residential qualifications. Once he has done so the advantages are considerable, because income tax is only 20p in the £1. There is no death duty, no capital gains tax and no VAT.

Finally if you have an accident or find that you need medical advice whilst on holiday a visit to the doctor will cost you a small fee. If you need to stay in hospital, there is a reciprocal arrangement with the Mainland National Health Authorities, to treat serious cases free of charge.

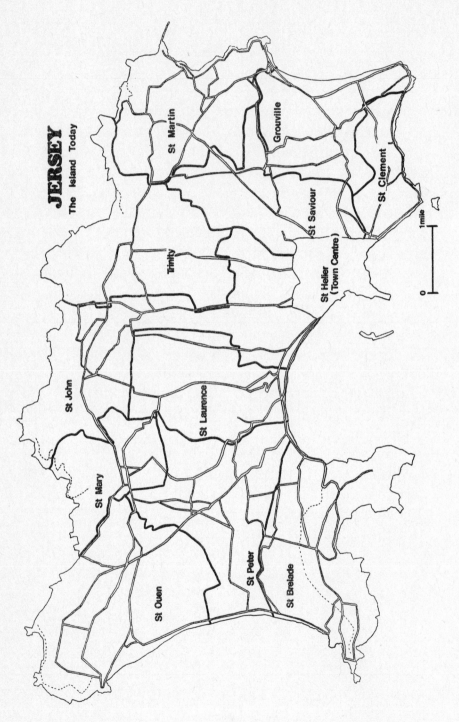

JERSEY
The Island Today

St Martin

Grouville

St Saviour

St Clement

Trinity

St Helier
(Town Centre)

St John

St Laurence

St Mary

St Ouen

St Peter

St Brelade

1 mile

0

Part I
Jersey

The Island Today

Jersey is the largest of the group of Channel Islands and measures 45 square miles. Although in 1980 Guernsey claimed to have received more visitors, Jersey has the reputation of being the chief tourist island. It has a varied landscape and in the north the coast line is rocky, in the south the land gently slopes to the beaches, which run into the sea as a shelf of smooth golden sand. The waves which roll in here last touched the shores of the Gulf of Mexico. The island is tailor made for holiday makers and **St Helier** is the chief centre for tourism. The whole of the south coast is lined with smart hotels and a few high rise buildings which give the town some of the character of a Mediterranean resort. It is hardly surprising that the island is such a popular holiday venue.

St Helier has developed from a small fishing village in to a busy commercial port. In summer it is a thriving district attracting visitors from all over the Continent, as well as Britain. The variety of things to be bought here includes: jewellery, alcohol, clothing and island produce. During the height of summer it is a buzzing centre of activity with traffic nearly bursting the seams of its modest one way system. Next to tourism Jersey is said to hold banking as the largest source of its revenue. On a stroll through the town centre you will see the names of most major banking corporations displayed grandly on gleaming brass plates or imposing carved stone plaques. There is no Value Added Tax here and it is easy to see why so many people return annually.

North of **St Helier** and away from the bustling activity of the south coast, quiet winding lanes lead you to peaceful fields. Here is the most likely place to come face to face with the famous Jersey cow. Exploration during the summer or during paler winter months will yield a rich return. Many of the charming granite farm houses have been renovated by 'immigrant islanders' and restored to peak condition. There are also a few cases where the original character of a building has been sacrificed in favour of lavish alteration. The island has a prosperous ambiance which sometimes can appear ostentatious, particularly when you catch sight of twin Rolls Royces parked in a driveway. Wealth is also reflected in immaculate gardens which are impeccably landscaped in a way which suggests that only a skilled gardener could possibly find the time or the expertise to look after them. But this feeling of care and attention to detail extends to the whole island. It always looks clean and pretty, especially in spring time when many of the green open spaces are covered with stunning yellow gorse and the grassy common is speckled with wild violets.

Much of the island appears the same as it did a century or two ago. A unique feature are the waterways carved through the countryside in valleys lined with lush trees. They are ideal to walk through on a sunny afternoon. Another of Jersey's unusual aspects are the cötils. These are steep valley faces used by farmers as agricultural land to produce plentiful seasonal crops; many can be seen in northern parts of the island particularly around **Rozel**

ST HELIER
The Town Centre

○ CAR PARKING

★ WC'S

Harbour. Jersey is divided into parishes which are each symbolised by a distinctive crest. These divisions can be traced back to medieval times. The closed island community which existed in the last century has opened up to new influences and today many of the residents have families who spend most of their time on the mainland occasionally coming back for holidays. The tourism which began in the mid-nineteenth century has increased the traffic of visitors to and from the island. Many of the old customs have been threatened as a result. One tradition is the Jersey Patois which the locals call 'Jersiase'. This is a mixture of Norman and French which can still be heard muttered on the odd street corner. These islanders are distinguishable by accent but are fast becoming few and far between. You may even see them mimicked in certain tourist publications or amusing cartoon strips for sale in the local newsagents.

SOME POINTS IN FAVOUR
Friendly local people, although slightly more distant than on the other islands. A variety of beaches for swimming and countryside for walking. 'Jersey Wonders' – ask for one in a local patisserie and take what you get for a genuine local snack. The pubs have extended drinking hours. Hours are from 9.00 am – 11.00 pm daily except on Sundays when they close from 2.00 pm – 5.00 pm. Exceptionally cheap wine and spirits, at least one third down on UK prices. Cheaper petrol although no doubt this is bound to increase. Accessible cheap shops and no VAT to add to your restaurant or hotel bills. Position close to the Continent with easy access to France. Excellent variety of food ranging from the usual English to French or Italian and even Chinese.

SOME POINTS AGAINST

In order to see the island a hired car is a must unless you can afford to bring your own. Inefficient transport system. Buses are infrequent and local timetables change seasonally. A Tourism Committee that prefers to hand out a barrage of leaflets and miscellaneous data rather than handle individual queries openly and conscientiously.

WHAT TO BRING

If you leave anything at home do not worry as most things are available here. Newspapers and magazines are the same as on the mainland and do not be surprised if you are asked to pay an extra penny per copy. The wind can be sharp. Anoraks and pullovers are a must. Beach things and towels and spades for the beaches. Tough shoes and warm clothes for walking along the cliffs or occasional birdwatching or just having a look at a local monument.

A Short History

The facts of Jersey history do not seem spectacular when read off like a shopping list. However most of the shopping you may be doing will be on a site that has changed dramatically since it was first established.

When the history of Jersey began as we know it today, bartering may have been the only means of exchange. Besides the remains that have been unearthed little is known about the early island communities. La Cotte de St Brelade is a site on the south west point of Jersey where human and animal remains have been discovered, as well as flint and stone tools. For early man was an inventor by necessity and his ingenuity is apparent when you visit La Hougue Bie in Grouville on the south east side of the island. This passage grave consists of a tunnel lined with granite which opens out into a large chamber. An earth mound was originally built to cover it that was so high that for centuries nobody knew why it was there. The site was considered pagan and many attempts were made to Christianise it. A chapel was built on the summit during the 12th century said to have been dedicated to a medieval knight according to local legend. Another was built by the Dean of Jersey during the 15th century when the life of a religious pilgrim was in vogue and buildings were erected for the Greater Glory of God. Thanks to the excavating efforts of La Société Jersiaise the grave is now uncovered and open to the public.

Another ancient site which lies to the north west of the island is Pinnacle Rock or Le Pinacle which was used as a place of settlement for over 2,000 years. Early communities flourished here, and later the site was used as a Gallo-Roman Temple.

Throughout the Roman Empire the Channel Islands formed a part of Gaul. It seems that the Romans did not feel at home in Jersey for there are few remains that indicate prolonged settlement. It is more likely that they governed the local inhabitants by extracting taxes and using the island as a trading station between Gaul, England and Ireland, valuing the island for its fortunate strategic position rather than any natural charm, like the Britons, French and Germans that followed them.

By the 6th century Christianity had reached the islands. St Brendan is said to have landed here and built a church but the main saint associated with the island is St Helier. This is the man who gave his name to Jersey's main town and to whom the parish church of St. Helier is dedicated. He is also perhaps the first and only saint to have a well built in his honour! The story of how this came about is well worth relating.

St Helier was a native of Tongues in Limburg, in the Netherlands, who travelled to Jersey and became a hermit. Unfortunately the Jersey people had not developed the sense of hospitality then that they show today, as in AD 555 St Helier met a savage death at the hands of local heathens. One of his last wishes, prompted no doubt by his untimely end was to be buried in Beville, Normandy which is far away from the fateful scene of the crime. Accordingly, his body was encased in a heavy stone coffin and carried across the island towards a waiting ship. When the overworked water bearers passed the site where St Helier's church is now standing, they dropped their load to the ground - and immediately a spring of clear fresh water gushed from the spot. Subsequently a well was built which can still be seen today.

POLITICS AND WAR

For the last ten centuries Jersey has been subject to invasion and interference from it's nearest neighbours, namely England, France and Germany. From the 9th century onwards the Vikings swept down to raid Europe from Scandinavia. At first their main objective was to plunder the land and rape the natives, but later they settled in the northern part of Gaul which was later to become Normandy. The 'Norsemen' as the locals probably referred to them introduced the name of Jersey as we know it today; the Norse word for island is 'Ey'. By the mid 10th century Charles the Simple bestowed the Channel Islands on one of these Viking descendants who was then the current Duke of Normandy, Rollo.

Norman rule continued unbroken for approximately 100 years. The islanders found themselves at the mercy of foreign Dukes, the successors of Rollo who had earned nicknames which supposedly matched their prowess. First there was Duke Richard 'the Fearless' who was succeeded by Duke Richard 'the Good'. After this righteous spell the Duchy was ruled by Duke Robert, known as 'the Devil' by some and 'the Magnificent' by others, depending upon your point of view. He is said to have landed in Jersey whilst sailing between Normandy and England because of bad weather. According to one legend he also had Edward the Atheling as a royal passenger, history has named him

31

Edward the Confessor! Lastly, Duke William was unfortunately dubbed 'the bastard' until he visited England in 1066. His luck changed when he defeated King Harold at Hastings and from that moment onward he was known as 'the Conqueror'.

This period was historically significant for all the Channel Islands. The Norman victory transferred possession of English lands to a joint Anglo Norman state. The political association which was formed has continued almost unbroken to the present day which makes the Channel Islands one of the oldest parts of the Commonwealth. But shadows of the Norman-Viking influence still remain, not only from the name of the island itself but also in many existing island traditions which date back to early Norman institutions.

A further development in the history of the island was the invasion of Normandy by King Philip of France in 1202. This loss has always been attributed to King John who luckily realised the strategic importance of keeping the small pieces of land in the Channel as part of his dominion. From being a relatively peaceful group of islands they were suddenly plunged into a state of perpetual war and were quite unprepared for the attack. England and France were at war for the next 150 years. They argued over the right to possess Normandy, they argued over Edward II's right to the French throne; sometimes they argued over who was to get the Channel Islands; more often than not they merely took the opportunity to seize and control. The islands had become pawns in a game of international chess. The allegiance of many islanders became divided since some of the Norman families who had settled on the islands still possessed land in Normandy. A decision had to be made on whether to remain on the islands or return to the mainland. Most of

32

them acted according to their best financial interests and the few remaining families were to have quite an influence over island affairs.

But all this became too much for the Jersey people. Internal disruption and cross-Channel antagonism forced them to take themselves, their livestock and the pitifully few valuables they retained to hide in the island's castles. These provided woefully inadequate protection without organised troops to man them. Punished beyond endurance, in 1294 they petitioned England's Privy Council for assistance against the continual onslaught of French attacks and for a reprieve from heavy taxation (imposed to aid the mainland war effort) which made the bad situation even more intolerable. It was not until 1335 that the Crown commissioned John de Roches to train men in the island's defence. Under his command, fortifications were built, soldiers were trained, but the new army was weak security against organised French might, and any relief was spasmodic.

One of the most notorious of Jersey's many assailants throughout the endless war years was a Castilian called Count Pierro Nino from Buelna, who took St Helier Priory at L'Islet, near to St Aubin's Bay by storm in 1406. The islanders were desperate to achieve peace at any cost and they eventually managed to bribe the Count to leave at considerable cost with 10,000 gold crowns, plus an annual tribute of 12 lances, 12 battle axes, 12 bows, 12 arrows and 12 trumpets!

Following the 100 Year's War in 1483, Edward IV persuaded the Church to grant the Channel Islands a Papal Bull of Neutrality in times of war to guarantee some degree of peace. The Bull was not always respected, but it did enable the islanders to found a healthy merchant economy. For over 200 years until William of Orange repealed the grant to prevent enemies of England finding political sanctuary in the islands, Jersey inhabitants were left relatively free to look after their own affairs. War continued to preoccupy the mainland but changing religious beliefs and continued heavy taxation were by and large the only aspects of English rule to interfere with day-to-day life.

In the early 17th century, during the English Civil War, the Channel Islands were once again infected by mainland rivalries. Loyalties within the islands became divided. In contrast to Guernsey, the majority of Jersey's leading families backed the Royalist cause against Parliament and under their power and influence the whole island undertook to support the Crown. Sir Philip Carteret, ardent Royalist and Bailiff at the time played host to the fugitive Charles II and was one of the many residents who had cause to regret the death of King Charles I. After the Parliamentary victory, his influential enemies submitted 15 articles of complaint alleging that he had grossly mismanaged island affairs to Parliament in England, and as a result a Committee of Lords and Commons replaced Sir Philip with five island Commissioners, under a new Lord of the Islands, Robert Earl of Warwick.

But all loyalty has it's reward. On his accession to the English throne, Charles II bestowed property and titles on many Jersey residents. Sir Philip Carteret received lands in America among which was Smiths Island, later renamed New Jersey and later populated by pilgrims emigrating to the New World. He and his son became 'Keepers of Our Game Within and About Our Said Isle of Jersey during your lives and the Life of the Longer liver of you'. This order included the protection of the hares, rabbits, partridges and wild fowl on the island. Hunting became so popular that an Act was later passed in 1668 forbidding the shooting of game to ensure the survival of the island wildlife which made this title redundant. Other members of the family were given the remaining Sanctuary paths and wastelands on the island. For the Jersey people as a whole, there was an emblem of enduring thanks - the silver mace which Jersey Bailiffs still carry before them at sittings in the Royal Court.

A diary written at this time by Jerseyman and ardent Royalist John Chevalier still survives in St Helier Museum. It is also available in the original French as published by La Société Jersiaise. Another notable inhabitant of Jersey at this time was Thomas Pepys, uncle of the famous diarist Samuel Pepys, who spent much time in Jersey in the company of Charles II.

The Stuart reign was a peaceful one and life on Jersey centred around the quiet pursuits of knitting, cidermaking, fishing and farming. Twice, during the turn of the century, the islanders feared that they might become involved in European wars - and many fortifications were constructed at this time. The first false alarm was occasioned by the French Revolution which sent hundreds of French Royalists scurrying to safety in Jersey. Despite the fact that by 1789 the island's population was one fifth French fugitive, the revolutionary antagonism did not stretch that far. A decade later, Fort Regent was built in anticipation of more trouble from the Napoleonic wars. The island fears were confirmed when the French made what was to be their final attempt to capture the islands in 1782. They were defeated, and this decisive victory for the English has been known ever since as the Battle of Jersey. It removed further threats of invasion, and ironically neither the fort which is now a vast amusement park, nor St. Catherines Harbour which was built with the original intention of sheltering Nelson's fleet have ever been put to the use for which they were originally intended. Both however, were used by the Germans as defence in the Second World War.

THE WAR YEARS

The German invasion on July 1st 1940 marked the end of over a century of peaceful self reliance for the Jersey islanders. Those that remained found themselves living under an enemy occupation which was to last nearly five years. Many of the islanders had chosen to leave the island for the Mainland realising that war was imminent. The Royal Jersey Militia left the island at this time and the Lieutenant Governor was withdrawn with them. The Bailiffs took the place of the governor and in Jersey a Superior Council was set up to carry out island affairs. In Guernsey a Controlling Committee was established for the same purpose. The first German Commander in Chief of the Channel Islands was Colonel Graf von Schmettow who started to refortify the island immediately. Monuments from the wartime occupation are still visible, La Rue du Nord is a road, built on the north of the island, by prisoners of war is still the widest road on the island today.

Other monuments include numerous bunkers and also a underground hospital which was intended by the Germans to be used as a place for wounded troops brought over from France to recover in but was never put to use. Food during the war was severely rationed. Examples of the island black market prices are tea which was available at £18-£25 a pound and one pound of butter cost as much as £2.2s. Bicycling became the main form of transport since petrol rationing was so severe. Foreign prisoners were imported as a labour for all the building work on the island. Mr. Coutanche was the island Bailiff and was later made a Lord for his expert handling of island affairs during the time that the island was occupied.

A German Official newpaper was circulated in the island called Deutsche Inzelzeit, in Guernsey it's counterpart was called 'Deutsche Zeitung'. Reichskredit marks were issued as special currency which represented Reichmarks but these were forbidden to circulate in Germany. After two years the pressure was increased on the islanders by a ban on wireless sets which was introduced in June 1942. Some people evaded this order by constructing their own 'cats whiskers' or crystal sets which enabled many of the islanders to listen to outside broadcasts. A few people ignored it, but the penalty for being discovered was severe. Canon Cohu, Rector of St Saviour was one of them and was immediately sentenced to 4 years imprisonment. He died in Spergau Concentration Camp. In September of the same year further precautions were taken by the Germans and any one living on the islands who had been born elsewhere in the British Isles were forcibly removed and sent to Germany. They were placed in internment camps for the remainder of the war. Penalties for offences were severe, a twenty-year-old Frenchman and his friends were captured in Guernsey as the beginning of the war attempting to join the Free French Forces. They had landed mistaking the island for the Isle of Wight and were imprisoned. Their leader Francois Scornet was shot by firing squad and 4 of his friends died in prison under appalling conditions. Anyone attempting to harbour prisoners received harsh sentences. Three Channel Islanders were imprisoned for helping a young Todt worker who was on the run. One of them, Mrs Gould, died in Ravensbrûck Concentration Camp and her brother Harry Osmond Le Druillenec miraculously survived imprisonment in Belsen.

Although their allies on the mainland were powerless to help them, the Red Cross were allowed to send shipments of supplies to the islanders which saved them on a number of occasions as they became pitifully short of food. Some of the islanders' attempts to provide themselves with some sort of luxury can be seen at La Hougue Bie Museum including some home-grown tobacco.

Morale on the islands were low but spirits were raised whenever news from home filtered through on an illegally held radio. On Guernsey a makeshift newsletter was compiled every day except Sunday which was printed on tomato packaging paper. The publication was called 'GUNS' which stood for 'Guernsey underground news service. News was received via BBC news bulletins and up to 780 words were written on average each day. At the top of the newsletter was printed the letters GUNS and V for Victory. The system went unnoticed until 1944 when an informer betrayed the 5 editors responsible. They were all imprisoned in Germany and received sentences ranging from 10 months to two years and four months. Only three survived the ordeal.

On the mainland, apart from Cummunications handled by the Red Cros, 'The Channel Islands Monthly Review' gave refugees news of their relatives on the islands. A Channel Islands Refugee Committee was set up for the few islanders who are known to have escaped. After the Allied Invasion into Europe on 6 June 1944 the German Occupation on the islands became even more tense. Schmettow was replaced by Vice Admiral Hüffmeier in February 1945, a staunch Nazi who clamped down on the islanders even harder than his predecessor had done. In retaliation, cases of sabotage were reported on Jersey at the Place Hotel, at St Saviour's and even at a Todt workers depot.

By 19th May 1945 it was clear that the occupation was nearly over and on 8th May the Islands were relieved by two destroyers, the Beagle and the Bulldog, which carried out the famous liberation of the Channel Islands in an exercise called 'Operation Nest Egg'.

After the war the British Nationality Act restored the Channel Islands to their former status. Today visitors to the island are still faced with frequent reminders of the occupation. Throughout the strains and stringencies imposed by the Occupation the island people have retained the sense of pride and defiance that has earned them the special place in the British Commonwealth which they hold today. Nowadays, when things are considerably quieter it seems strange to remember that the Battle of Hastings was just over 900 years ago, and although life in comparison may seem a little tame, it certainly suits the people better.

TRADE, TOURISM & RELIGION

From early days, religion and ecclesiastical ways dominated almost every facet of island life. Inhabitants were not only locked into an endless round of religious observances, but also subject to the authority of the Church in most matters of law and administration. By the 12th century much of the island's land was the property of religious houses who invariably came from overseas. The Bishop of Coutances held a manor in Jersey, and with it the right to collect half the taxes paid to the Parish of St Saviour, and the Biship of Avrances owned a manor in St John's Parish as well as land in Trinity. Day-to-day administration – of taxes was also determined by the Church; in the Parish or Ecclesiastical Court.

The power of the Church at this time can be illustrated

by the following anecdote. In 1203, just a few years after King John had consolidated his hold over the Channel Islands, England donated the Ecrehous Islands to the Abbey Val Richter in Normandy. The gift was not an entirely selfless one, for it was a medieval belief that property given to the Church would ensure the donor a place in heaven. Repeatedly throughout the island's history, the Church was evoked as the fount of all justice and wisdom; it was also called upon to protect its subjects. In 1331 the Prior of St Clement on Jersey was asked to protect the island's liberty and ancient rights against the abuse of fines. His success in this matter may be in doubt, but for proof of the very real power wielded by the pre-Reformation Church, one has merely to remember that a Papal Bull of Neutrality granted in 1483 achieved 200 years of relative peace and protection for Jersey traders.

Following the granting of a Papul Bull, the Jersey people were able to establish a healthy economy based on the exchange of wool, cloth, hides, metal and grain for cargoes of wine and spices from Gascony. Fishing for conger and mackeral also flourished.

In 1547 Henry VIII broke all ties with Rome and instituted his Divine Service. (A letter of thanks from the Privy Council to the Jersey people in 1549 proves that they obligingly adopted this replacement for the Mass). The effect that this had on the islanders at the time is unclear; punishments were meted out to recalcitrants found in possession of a rosary or practising Mass, but there are no recorded deaths. Today, however, the lasting effect that the Reformation had on the island's history is sadly evident in the few religious relics, chapels and even original church bells that survived its period.

In 1550 Royal Commissioners were appointed to sell all Church property on behalf of the Crown. Stained glass windows, fonts and all other signs of so-called Popery were destroyed. Henry's priorities were obvious: the proceeds of his demolition went towards defence and filling the Privy Purse. (Altar Stones were even incorporated in alterations being carried out on Mount Orgeuil Castle.)

Not unnaturally, the fall of the established Church was accompanied by a decline in priestly morals. Hypocrisy was rife, as illustrated by the following story. In 1550 it was discovered that a priest named Richard Averty had strangled his illegitimate baby only hours after its mother, a long-standing household servant, has born it. One horrifying aspect of the tale lies in the fact that he considered it his duty to baptise the child. The incident has acquired notoriety in local folklore, and today you still hear islanders refer to a "Richard Averty Repentance", meaning one that has come too late.

Henry VIII was succeeded by "Bloody Mary" whose reign is characterised by the terrible punishments meted out to those who did not achieve the required level of outward religious piety. Fear, tension and distrust stimulated a rash of fanatical witch hunts which resulted in 66 official trials from 1562-1736 on Jersey alone. Retribution for the guilty varied, but Jersey's particular favourite was hanging followed by burning.

During the reign of Elizabeth I hundreds of French Hugenots escaped to Jersey with the result that Protestantism took a dominant hold. Protetantism has never been a particularly demanding religion and Elizabeth was an easy Queen; life became more pleasant for the islanders. In 1600 Sir Walter Raleigh was made Governor of Jersey and, under his command, fortifications were strengthened and Elizabeth Castle was erected. It was an age of dash and panache and, following the example of the mainland and indeed their Governor, Jerseymen took up a trade they had always been rather good at – piracy.

Up until the 16th century there had been little opportunity for Jersey's inhabitant to improve the quality of their lives. They had spent so much time and money merely protecting what they already had. But now, politics took a second place and the serious business of building towns and trade could begin.

Ironically, the Reformation was the original cause for improved social facilities on the island. As the strength of the Church declined, so its ability to provide help for the community increased. Grammar schools were built to the east and west of the island, and Jersey's first hospital was erected near the present site of La Hougue Bie Chapel. By the turn of the 18th century packet mail steamers were making regular trips between Weymouth and all the Islands, and in 1802 Jersey life was affluent and sophisticated enough to merit a theatre – the Theatre Royal, St Helier.

Throughout the 19th century communications continued to improve. Appallingly unhygenic and unpleasant open drains were replaced by proper underground sewers (after 348 people had died in two separate outbreaks of cholera); horse-drawn cabs were on the roads by 1850; in 1896 the first island telephone system was introduced. Three years later 'macadamisation' of Jersey's previously unnerving roads allowed the use of motorised transport; and, finally, in 1937 the island acquired an airport.

Today, Jersey has every amenity that you could wish. In fact, some aspects of Jersey life are considerably more sophisticated than on many parts of the mainland. Take banking, for example. Jersey has been an international monetary centre since 1797 when the island's first bank was established by Hugh Godfray, a wine merchant. By the mid-19th century the banks were doing so well that jealous complaints were raised against the "soi disant bankers" who took it upon themselves to issue private banknotes in the privacy of their own homes! It was cottage industry at its very best.

Incidentally, Jersey coinage was only introduced in 1841; before that it had been both French and English. The museum at St Helier devotes a section to the subject, and is well worth a visit.

If you read this short history of Jersey before you visit the island you will not fail to notice how strangely placid and peaceful it is in contrast to its active, not to say bloody, past. Indeed, the only battle likely to touch the visitor is the "Battle of Flowers" – an oddly warlike name for a happy annual festival held every summer to mark the coronation of Edward VII. No doubt Jersey likes it better that way.

Some Famous Inhabitants

THOMAS PEPYS: the uncle of diarist Samuel Pepys lived in Jersey during the reign of Charles II. Samuel Pepys visited the island from time to time and mentions it in his writings.

JOHN MILLAIS: was born in Jersey and painted the famous 'Bubbles' picture, which was originally intended as a portrait of his grandson William James. Once out of his hands the picture was later purchased by the company of Pears Soap, which to his horror was used extensively by them for advertising purposes.

VICTOR HUGO: escaped from France during the French Revolution and lived in Jersey for a short while. He was later expelled from the island in 1855 for openly criticising a state visit made by Queen Victoria to France. Later he went to live in Guernsey.

ANTHONY TROLLOPE: began his career as a clerk and was later employed by the Jersey Post Office. He was probably involved in organising the introduction of pillar boxes to the island in 1852. None of these original post boxes remain to be seen in Jersey today.

LILLIE LANGTRY: her real name was Emilie Charlotte Le Breton and she was born the daughter of a clergyman. She became famous not only as a society beauty, but also as an actress and was a contemporary of Oscar Wilde, as well as the painter Rex Whistler. Millais also painted a portrait of her holding a lily and the name of the painting 'Jersey Lily' became her nickname during the development of her career. She died in 1929 and is buried in St Saviour's churchyard.

MARY ANN EVANS: is better known as George Eliot. She lived quietly for some weeks at Rose Cottage, now known as Villa Rosa, in Gorey Village during the summer of 1857.

ELEANOR GLYN: born late in the 19th century lived to become a script writer who worked during the first golden days of Hollywood.

How to get to the Island

by air p45   by sea p47   by rail p47   by car p48   by coach p49   animals on the ferry p49

By Air

As well as being the largest of the four major Channel Islands Jersey also has the finest airport, which is large and spacious. Polished chrome and luminous orange perspex notices gleam with authority, and visitors are greeted with as much slick efficiency as in any major international airport. The large number of airlines operating from all over Europe reinforce this impression. Every morning pin-striped businessmen walk briskly to or from their scheduled flights, armed with brief cases and the morning newspaper. For some it is cheaper to commute across the Channel than to pay English taxation. Whatever the reason business must be thriving and when travelling by air you may find yourself sitting next to one of them on any of the following flights: British Caledonian, Dan Air, KLM Airlines, Jersey European, British Midland, British

Airways, Aurigny Air Services, Air UK, Guernsey Airlines, Brymon Airways, Haywards Airways, Air Anglia, British Island Airways and Intra Airways. Expect to pay between £70-80 for a return flight.

A popular method of flying to Jersey used by locals travelling to the mainland is by train from London (Waterloo) to Southampton and then on by air to Jersey. Standby tickets are available on most flights in off peak seasons. During the winter some airlines cease operating altogether. For details, contact the individual airlines concerned or check with your local travel agent. Other items worth checking before you buy your ticket are reductions offered by some airlines for: advance bookings, student travel, group fares, members of HM forces, or standby flights.

Visitors to Jersey from the mainland do not need to bring a passport. However if you intend to travel to France during your stay it is necessary to have either your passport, or a '24 hour identity card', which is available on request from ticket offices at a small cost, providing you remember to bring 2 passport sized photographs of yourself with you. For visitors from Europe and elsewhere the same rules of entry apply to Jersey as to the United Kingdom. The Passport Office for renewals or any queries is at:

Victoria Chambers, Conway Street, St Helier. Offices open Monday - Friday 9.00-1.00 pm and 2.00-4.30 pm.

International visitors must first fly to Heathrow or Gatwick and change flights to get to Jersey. The following airlines operate direct from Paris:

Air UK, 6 Caledonia Place, St Helier, Tel: Jersey 41111
Jersey European Airways, 10 Conway St, St Helier, Tel: Jersey 77400
Aurigny Air Services run regular flights to Cherbourg

contact:
Town Office, 6 Caledonia Place, St Helier, Tel: Jersey 35733
Flights to Belgium or Brest, Dinard, Granville, St Brieuc and Deauville are also run by Jersey European Airways.

By Sea

The Sealink Service provides car and passenger ferries which depart from Portsmouth or Weymouth. During the summer sailings are twice a day from Weymouth and only once a day from Portsmouth. During winter, services are restricted to once a day from Weymouth and every other day from Portsmouth except during Christmas week when the service shuts down. The price for an adult return ticket is £37 return from Weymouth or £41 return from Portsmouth.

Rail

British Rail co-operate with the Jersey Tourist Board each year and produce various brochures advertising their holiday breaks in summer and winter. These are very reasonable and include the cost of travel and weekend bookings in a variety of Jersey hotels. There are special arrangements available according to the season. Night Flyer Awaydays are usually available from May to September which includes return Sealink travel, a bonus pack of Whiskey or Gin, two litres of wine, and travel overnight, arriving in Jersey early in the morning in time for breakfast. There is a coach tour of the island in the morning, and departure from the island back home at noon. For details of these or any other arrangements on offer contact Sealink or investigate through your local travel agent. An ordinary adult 3 monthly return rail ticket costs £54. Most British Rail fares are generally half price for children, students or old age pensioners. Midweek travelling is generally cheaper. Sealink sailings are daily from May-October.

By Car

Most people want to ensure that they have transport when they arrive for their holiday on the island. Car hire is available, but if you want to drive your own then Sealink offer the best terms for transporting cars and their passengers to the islands. The cost of transporting an average sized vehicle is £44 return. Trailer caravans are prohibited. Advance booking is essential. For Sealink bookings contact:
Sealink Car Ferries, PO Box 303, London SW1G 0AG, or Sealink UK Ltd., Weymouth Quay, Dorset, DT4 8DY, or Sealink UK Ltd., Norman House, Kettering Terrace, Portsmouth, PO2 7AE.
For further enquiries tel: 01 834-2345.

By Coach

The National Coach Service provides the cheapest form of travel from London to Portsmouth or Weymouth for under £5. Bookings are in advance and standby tickets are also available for as little as £2.00. Enquiries to:
The National Coach Service, Victoria Coach Station, 164 Buckingham Palace Road, London, SW1
For enquiries tel: 01 730-0202

Animals on the Ferry

Dogs are discouraged from travelling on the ferry. Cages or kennels have to be provided by passengers without cars. Dogs may be left in the cars during the crossing and at their owners risk and a cost of £7.50.

Inter-Island Travel

by air p50   by sea 51   services to the continent p51

By Air

Travelling between Jersey, Guernsey and Alderney by air is quicker, but more expensive than by any other form of travel. In the case of Alderney, flying is best as the crossing by sea can be very rough and the number of sailings are restricted in summer and stop completely in winter. For flights to and from Jersey to Guernsey, Alderney or France contact:

Aurigny Air Services Ltd, Town Office, Weighbridge, St Helier. tel: Jersey 35733

Flights between the islands are approximately £10 for single, or £15 return. A 3 day ticket costs approximately £16.

By Sea

Most people staying in Jersey are tempted to visit the other islands at some time or another, or make a trip to France as it is so close: Condor Commodor & Shipping Services Ltd, 28 Conway Street, Albert Quay, St Helier. tel: Jersey 71263 operate daily a hydrofoil service between the islands which runs twice a day during the summer. They also provide ferries between Jersey, Guernsey and St Malo and schedule two weekly sails to Alderney. There is also a currency exchange service for passengers to and from the Continent available from their offices in Conway Street, St Helier.

Sealink also operate a steamer between Jersey and Guernsey every day during the summer, which takes between 3 and 4 hours, and is a pleasant way of passing the day in fine weather. Their offices are at:
Sealink, West's Centre, Bath Street, St Helier. tel: Jersey 77122
For other day trips and excursions from Jersey contact:
Preston Travel, Colombiere Ltd,Dolphin House, Colombiere, St Helier. tel: Jersey 74111, or
Bellingham, 6 Caledonian Place,Weighbridge Street, St Helier. tel: Jersey 27841
For most passenger services it is advisable to arrive at the quayside at least 20 minutes before departure to avoid missing the boat.

Services to the Continent

During the summer, Condor run a hydrofoil service between Jersey and St Malo. Contact:

Condor Commodore and Shipping Services Ltd., 28 Conway Street, Albert Quay, St Helier, Tel: Jersey 71263 There are 6 daily sailings throughout the summer, between May and September. The service is reduced during the low season and shuts down completely between January and February. Prices are £11 single. £18 for a 72-hr ticket and £20 for a period ticket.

Marine Management, tel: Jersely 32407 run a car ferry from St Helier to St Malo between May and September. There are 2 sailings daily, 5 times a week. This service shuts down beteen January and February and there is a reduced service during the low season. Prices are £30 for a 10′ car, £60 return.

Marine Management also run a passenger boat called *The Belle de Jersey* which runs from St Helier to Granville between April and September. The boat leaves each evening and prices are £11 single, £20 return.

Travel within the Island

by car p54   by car hire p55   by taxi p56   by
motorcycle p56   by bicycle p57   by public
transport p57   island tours p58   by wheelchair p58
caravan p58

A visitor to the island in 1870 would have been delighted
to find that the Jersey Railway Company had recently
opened a line which ran from the **Weighbridge** in St
Helier to **St Aubin** on the opposite side of the Bay. In 1873
a rival the Jersey Eastern Railway Company opened
another railway which gave any traveller the chance to
travel eastwards in style to **Gorey Village**. By 1899 this
southern railway stretched from **Corbiere Point** in the
west to **Gorey** in the east. There were even tramways to be
seen in **St Helier** run by the Jersey Railways and Tran-
ways Ltd. Sadly, none of these forms of transport are
functioning on the island today and can only be seen as
museum pieces. Their introduction to Jersey was quickly
superceded by another novelty – that of motorised traffic.
Today there are any number of coaches and cars which
take you around the island to your destination. These may

seem less romantic but are definitely more practical, unless you want to be very independent and see the island by bicycle.

By Car

The Jersey speed limit is 40 mph – sometimes 20 mph in certain signposted areas. The best way to see the island is by car whether you intend to hire on or bring your own. The rules of the road are similar to those in England and the main differences are worth noting:

Minor roads are indicated by yellow lines painted across them.

When entering major roads from a minor one be sure that the road is clear.

Island roads are mostly narrow and there are danger spots to look out for.

If there is an accident the police must be informed.

Use of car horns between 11.00 pm and 6.00 am are restricted.

Motorcycles or bicycles must not be pushed or driven abreast on the roads.

No cars or vehicles are to be driven onto the beaches.

Traffic lights are similar to England excepting the stop to start signals which run straight through from red to green.

In summer the roads are crowded and in St Helier the traffic can be very congested. For this reason there is a one way system in town and a shortage of parking space. Jersey has a strict parking system which allows vehicles to park between 20 minutes and 3 hours in some areas. Circular discs with clock faces are issued so that they can be set at the time of leaving your car, and thus rechecked to indicate the time the vehicle has been left unattended. Discs are available automatically with cars hired on the island. Other visitors with their own cars may obtain discs from the town hall in St Helier, or the Motor Traffic Office in Pier Road, at 20p each.

Car Hire

Visitors intending to hire a car on the island must remember to bring their own driving licences. Garages will not hire out cars without a certificate of insurance and this needs a driving licence as proof of your identity. There are many car hire garages on the island and prices are generally fixed in the summer. Expect to pay between £8-£10 per day. All hire cars are identifiable by the 'H' which is next to the island number plates so it is unlikely that you will lose your way in the countryside! Also it means that all car driving visitors are easily identifiable, so leave any bad driving habits at home. Car hire is available from the following places:
Avis Rent-a-Car, Jersey Airport. tel: Jersey 42080
Godfrey Davis, Jersey Airport. tel: Jersey 43156
Conway Motors, 33 Gloucester Street, St Helier. tel: Jersey 33666
Holiday Hire Cars, 4 The Parade, St Helier. tel: Jersey 7398/20464
It is possible to book a car so that it is waiting on arrival by air or by sea. Some hotels include this service in their arrangements and many self catering houses offer cheap car hire included in their terms.

By Taxi

The taxis that run in Jersey are all licensed. Expect to pay 50p at the start plus additional mileage. They are available from:

Public Rank Taxi's, Weighbridge, St Helier. tel: Jersey 32001

Public Rank Taxi's, Broad Street, St Helier. tel: Jersey 23001

St Peter Airport. tel: Jersey 41420.

If there are any queries or any complaints these should be directed to the Motor Traffic Office, Pier Road, St Helier, Jersey.

By Motorcycle

To hire a motorcycle you must be aged over 20 and posses a clean current British Driving Licence or equivalent. Wearing a helmet is compulsory.

Hire of moped costs from £4 per day—£24 per week.

250cc motorcycles costs from £6 per day-£36 per week.

400cc motorcycles on hire from £45 per week – and you must be aged 25 or over.

These are for hire from:

Gryphon Garage, Pontac, St Helier, tel: Jersey 54534

Motorama Two Wheel Centre, 16 Don Road, St Helier, tel: 22819/20

By Bicycle

Bicycling is a popular way of exploring the island in fine weather, especially if you feel energetic. Visitors to the island on Easter Monday could join the local enthusiasts who throughout the day bicycle between pubs on a gigantic pub crawl. Bicycles are available for hire from the following establishments:

Kingslea Cars, 16 The Esplanade, St Helier. tel: Jersey 24777

Hire Ride, 1 St John's Road, St Helier. tel: Jersey 31995

The Hire Shop, St Aubin's Road, Millbrook. tel: 73699

Easy Ride, 23 Havre des Pas, St Helier. tel: 27968

Expect to pay a deposit which is refundable on return of the bicycle.

By Public Transport

Buses leave the Central Bus and Coach Station at the Weighbridge, St Helier at regular intervals. Timetables change seasonally and if you buy a current timetable it will save a lot of time waiting for some of the buses which only run at certain times of the day.

Island Tours

There are various coach tour operators on the island which offer morning, afternoon or day trips which combine conducted tours of the island with visits to places of interest. Cost varies from £3.50-£5.00. People to contact are:
Blue Coach Tours, 70-72 Columberie, St Helier. tel: Jersey 22584
Pioneer Coaches, Albert Street, St Helier. tel: Jersey 25100
Waverley Coaches Ltd, 10 Gloucester Street, St Helier. tel: Jersey 72962
Tantivy Motors Ltd, 10 Parade, St Helier. tel: Jersey 32383
Clarendon Coaches Ltd, 5 The Esplanade, St Helier. tel: Jersey 74242

By Wheelchair

If this is what you need to get about hire one from:
The Hire Shop, St Aubin's Road, Millbrook. tel: Jersey 73699
Cost £6.25 per week or £2.50 for the day. Incidentally, this shop also provides you with a roof-rack for your car at a cost of £1.50 per week.

Caravan

Trailer caravans are prohibited in Jersey, and dormobiles

and camper caravans need a special certificate of authority from Jersey Tourism Committee, but are not permitted for holiday purposes.

Where to Stay

hotels p62   guest houses p64   self catering accommodation p65   camping p66   holiday camps p68

One of the functions of the Jersey Tourism Committee is to provide factual information for visitors on where to stay on the island. Before you visit it is worth contacting the office to obtain the 'Official Holiday Accommodation List' and 'Information Digest' both of which are free on arrival or by post from:
The States of Jersey Tourism Committee, Tourist Information Office, Weighbridge, St Helier. tel: Jersey 78000.

There are 25,000 beds available in Jersey during the summer season which are filled annually. All the Hotels and Guest Houses on the Island are registered with the Committee. They have a strict grading system and premises are inspected regularly. This keeps a tight control on maintaining standards and at the same time gives an accurate picture of what visitors may expect to find when they come to stay for a holiday. All available accommodation on the island which has been inspected is registered and listed annually in the accommodation lists. Visitors can then choose for themselves the type of accommodation they are looking for to suit their needs and at a price they can afford. As in most provincial areas it is very much a case of 'you get what you pay for'. Many guest houses offer good value for money with comfortable surroundings and reasonable terms. Some offer half board accommodation which is ideal for couples or families who want to spend most of the day out on the beach.

Accommodation is divided into 2 categories: hotels and guest houses. The hotels in Jersey are divided into 2 classes which are First or Second Register according to the facilities they have to offer. First Register hotels offer the highest standards of accommodation which have to conform to strict controls and meet the regulatory checks of the Tourism Committee. They are represented by the symbol of the Four Suns. The number of Suns vary according to the standard offered within the particular category. Some hotels in this class offer the equivalent to RAC and AA with 3 or 4 star awards. The Second Register hotels are represented by the symbol of a diamond. Guest houses are smaller and more family orientated and most have a cosy caring atmosphere. One fact worth mentioning is that the smaller the number of people there are to look after, the greater the care and attention there is likely to be per head.

Since accommodation in Jersey is very limited during the high season due to the sheer volume of visitors (over 1 million people visited the island in 1980), it is advisable to ring well in advance of your holiday to make sure you get the type of accommodation you want. Although the Holiday Accommodation Booklet offers a good guideline on what you will get for your money, extra investigation is advisable to determine whether the hotel or guest house concerned is going to provide the quality you may be looking for. Points to check are:

1. Car parking facilities
2. Proximity to shops
3. Availability of public transport
4. Suitability for children
5. Additional facilities on offer: ie. Swimming pool etc.

Hotels

The following are a selection of hotels and guest houses on the island chosen because of their proximity to the beaches: Prices given are an approximate indication of what to expect for a single person staying at 'half-board' per day, as most hotel prices vary according to the time of year, those given are for the low as well as the high season, and are only approximate.

Rozel Bay-St Martin
This is one of the prettiest villages in Jersey. The harbour and fortifications here were built during the Napoleonic Wars.

LE COUPERON DE ROZEL HOTEL – First Register 3 Suns tel: Jersey 62190.
This is an attractive looking place to stay and has been successfully converted from a Napoleonic Fortress. As well as being within easy reach of the beach it has a swimming pool and is recommended for its sea food. Expect to pay

between £16-24.50 per day: bed, breakfast and evening meal.

LE PETITE CHAIRE GUEST HOUSE – Grade A. tel: Jersey 62682

This is a very attractive looking guest house which is only 50 yards from the beach. Extremely good value at £11.50 per day: bed breakfast and evening meal. Closed October-May.

St Catherines Bay – St Martin

LES ARCHES HOTEL – First Register 3 Suns tel: Jersey 53829

Also mentioned by the AA and RAC, this is a modern hotel with a good view of the Bay. It has a swimming pool, bar and car parking facilities. There is also a discotheque during the high season. £17.50-£22.00 bed, breakfast and evening meal. Closed January and Febraury.

Grouville Bay – Grouville

Near Mont Orgeuil Castle and overlooking the sandy bay are several places to stay near this pretty harbour.

GROUVILLE BAY HOTEL – First Register 3 Suns tel: Jersey 51004

This large reputable hotel over looks a golf course and is set back about 100 yards from the sea. It has a heated swimming pool as well as a good bar with dancing during the season. £15.00-£18.00 bed, breakfast and evening meal. Closed October-April.

MOORINGS HOTEL – First Register 2 Suns tel: Jersey 53633

This is a small period hotel and one of the many establishments built overlooking the harbour. It is well known for its good though pricey sea food and is frequented by locals. £19.50-£24.00 bed, breakfast and evening meal. Open all the year round.

Guest Houses

The following list of guest houses are open all the year round in Jersey. They are all grade 'A' establishments and the prices quoted are daily terms per person for bed, breakfast and evening meal. Open all the year round.

Bays, St Johns Road, St Helier, Jersey, tel: Jersey 24795, £10.50-£13.00.
Burleigh, 63 St Saviours Road, St Helier, tel: Jersey 30907, £8.00-£11.50.
Glenthorne, Elisabeth Place, St Helier, tel: Jersey 22817, £9.50-£12.00.
Greenwood Lodge, Roserville Street, St Helier, tel: Jersey 32215, £8.00-£12.60.
Leadon, 96 St Saviours Road, St Helier, tel: Jersey 24593, £7.00-£9.60.
Les Sablons, Beach Road, St Helier, tel: Jersey 32205, £7.50-£9.00.
Runnymede Court, Roseville Street, St Helier, tel; Jersey 20044, £8.00-£14.20.
Cutty Shark, Five Mile Road, St Ouen, tel: Jersey 81940, £11.00-£11.50.
Rockhampton, St Aubin's Road, St Aubin, tel: Jersey 24034, £8.50-£13.25.
Rosadella, Maufaut, St Saviour, tel: Jersey 53271, £10.50-£12.75.

White Heather, Rue du Haut, Millbrook, tel: Jersey 20430, £8.50-£11.60.
Richelieu Lodge, Bagot Road, St Saviour, tel: Jersey 31108, £8.20-£11.40.

The following grade 'A' guest houses provide bed and breakfast only and are open all the year round.

Mimosa, 94 St Saviour Road, St Helier, tel: Jersey 34137, £9.90-£12.30.
Monaco, 14 Parade Road, St Helier, tel: Jersey 24663, £7.25-£9.50.
Pentland Lodge, 43 St Saviours Road, St Helier, tel: Jersey 31719, £8.00-£9.00.
Southampton, Weighbridge, St Helier, tel: Jersey 20114, £8.00-£10.00.
Alfriston, Rue des Landes, St Peter, tel: Jersey 421704, £9.00-£9.25.
Bryn-y-Mor, La Haule, St Brelade, tel: Jersey 20295, £7.00-£9.15.
Charmel, St Aubin's Road, St Aubin, tel: Jersey 21135, £8.50-£9.00.
Sunseeker, Bagot Ra Road, St Saviour, tel: Jersey 76611, £7.75-£8.25.
Villa Ronceray, St Martin, tel: Jersey 52230, £8.00-£8.50.

Self Catering Accommodation

This is becoming increasingly popular. Many people are finding that they relax most when they can 'do their own thing'. This is particularly true for anybody who dislikes schedules, has a family, or particularly values their privacy. Self catering accommodation is limited on the island because rented accommodation is scarce and in great demand from permanent residents, and restrictions are imposed by the States on others to ensure that they have first choice. Consequently the States Tourism Committee does not publish information on self catering accommodation although some estate agents in St Helier do have houses on their books. One way of finding out if what you want is available is to advertise in the local newspaper *The Jersey Evening Post*. Contact:

The Advertising Dept, Charles Street, St Helier tel: Jersey 73333.

Camping

To some people camping offers an exciting alternative. To others it could summon up visions of a domestic nightmare under cover. However one fact is clear: that it is a cheap alternative to staying in any hotel, and during the summer, when the prospect of good weather is most likely, there are several sites on the island allocated for this purpose. For people with a natural inclination to steer clear of organised sites beware. The States do not take kindly to people pitching a tent without special permission from the owner of the property concerned. Camping is popular during the summer and advanced booking is necessary for most sites, so be sure to check this before you turn up, it will save you spending a night underneath the hedges with the Jersey cows for company. Each site stipulates camp rules which are made to regulate the volume of noise and general behaviour. Compared to many camping site on the Continent rules are more strict in Jersey. There are no caravan sites on the island and trailer tents are only allowed on registered sites. If you wish to bring a dormobile or camper caravan, a special certificate of authority must be obtained from Jersey Tourism Committee.

The sites

BEAUVELANDE – St Martin tel: Jersey 53575

This site measure approximately 100 yards square. Cars may be parked next to the tents. The surface is made up of earth track roads and a combination of grass and gravel. Facilities: TV room, games room, washroom, loos, small swimming bath for children, seesaw and slide. The shop opens daily between 8.00-12.30 am and 1.30-7.30 pm. Equipment for hire. Prices range from £1.50-£3.50 per person per day. Special rates for children.

ST BRELADES CAMPING PARK – Off Routes des Genets tel: Jersey 41398

Large well equipped site which stipulates couples or families only. Parking space available.

Facilities: washing facilities, loos, children's playpen, cafe on terrace and a shop. Equipment for hire. Prices range from £2.00-£3.00 per person per day.

QUENNEVAIS – St Brelade tel: Jersey 42436

This site is near to the airport and is medium sized. There is a modern building nearby with a helpful management. Facilities include: large concrete parking space, restaurant, games room, lounge, TV room, loos and a shop. Equipment for hire £1.50-£1.80 per day.

ROSE PARK – St Brelade tel: Jersey 41231
This camping site is on a hillside. Rough tracks lead to various sections, so that tents are on different levels. Parking spaces available beside tents.
Facilities: washing facilities, loos, TV room, shop, phone kiosk. Equipment for hire. Package Deal Holidays now available. £1.20 per person per day. Children half price. Closed October–May.

Holiday Camps

There are two holidays camps in Jersey.

PONTINS HOLIDAY CAMP – Plemont. tel: Jersey 81873
This is an entertainment complex composed of individual chalets which are situated around a main communal area. For anyone who wants to take themselves or their family to one place and not have to move out of it, this may be ideal for you. The facilities on offer here include bars, swimming pools and comfortable accommodation with a good sea view. There is a beach below which is accessible from the cliffs via a steep flight of steps. There is also entertainment in the evening which varies seasonally. Prices ranges from £58–£110 per person weekly. Price includes bedroom with bathroom plus 3 meals daily and evening entertainment. Closed October–April.

JERSEY HOLIDAY VILLAGE – Portelet. tel: Jersey 45555.
This is built on the side of a hill with a magnificent view. The hotel block has lifts and the rooms have bathrooms attached. The facilities include a heated open air swim-

ming pool and the main block houses a dining room and also a bar. Prices ranges from £68.00-£97.00 per person weekly. Price includes bed, breakfast and evening meal plus evening entertainment. Closed November-April.

Eating and Entertainment

restaurants p70 tea for two p73 dancing p75 pubs 75

Jersey is renowned for it's good food. Being an island so close to France the fact that French Cuisine and Seafood are both specialities is hardly surprising. The following restaurants listed are selected from all over the island to suit a wide variety of tastes. Prices quoted are approximate and are for a meal per person including wine unless stated otherwise.

Restaurants

LE BISTRO PREMIER Cattle Streeet, St Helier tel: Jersey 35299
This upstairs restaurant has an Italian and French menu which is good value, with cheap wine in comfortable surroundings. There is also a vegetarian menu specially dreamed up by the chef. Typical choice of courses might be Prawn Cocktail followed by Steak including wine at £10

per head for dinner. Lunch menu for soup followed by main course costs £2.15 not including wine. Open all the year round.

LE SOUPE A L'OIGNON 78 New Street, St Helier tel: Jersey 74110
Good value for money and a French menu which is all beautifully cooked from fresh local produce. Like most of the good things in life be prepared for a long wait but in the end you will find that the waiting has been well worth it. You can eat here for as little as £5 per head or spend as much as £15-£20, it is a flexible à la carte menu.

MAURO'S La Motte Street, St Helier tel: Jersey 2017
A fairly expensive Italian and French restaurant which specialises in sea food and in fish dishes. Dinner prices £9-10 not including wine. Special lunchtime menu for £2.75. Open all the year round.

BISTRO FRERE DE BORSALINO Gorselands, Rozel tel: Jersey 61000
Very good value restaurant with bistro style French food. The menu is original – deep fried garlic mushrooms and fine home made soups are two examples. Lunch set menu £2.75 not including wine. Dinner from £9 per person, including wine.

COTE DU NORD HOTEL Rozel tel: Jersey 61171
Situated on the north coast of the island the restaurant in this hotel is well known for the variety of sea food dishes and good cooking. £7.25 for dinner and a lunch menu for £3.25 not including wine. Restaurant closes every Tuesday. Otherwise open all the year around.

SEASCALE HOTEL Gorey pier, tel: Jersey 54395
This is another restaurant with a reputation for its sea
food specialities and also with moderate prices to match.
Specialities de la Maison include: Fruites des Mers, turbots
and Moules Meuniere. A la carte menu only in the
evening. Lunch time set menu £3.30, £4.40 or £6.60.

LA BUKA RESTAURANT The Parade, St Helier, tel: Jersey
34283
This is the place to go to find good Italian food in comfortable surroundings. Dinner at £10 per head including
house wine. A good value lunchtime menu to be tried for
£3.00. Closed on Wednesdays during the winter season.

THE YANKEE RESTAURANT Bath Street, St Helier, tel: Jersey
37397
Jersey's answer to London's famous American Disaster
restaurant. Informal relaxed chequered tablecloths and a
good cheap hamburger style menu. Expect to pay
£4.50-£5.00 per head for lunch or dinner. Take away
service daily. Open all the year round.

THE ATLANTIC HOTEL La Pulente, St Brelade tel: Jersey
44101
Another hotel on the island with a reputation for providing
dishes cooked personally by the chef with an excellent sea
food menu. £10 per head for dinner. £6.00 at lunchtime.
Closed January-March.

PORTOFINO RESTAURANT St Aubins, tel: Jersey 42100
Very good for Italian style food. Set menu at lunchtime
from between £3-£4 not including wine. Set dinner from
£5.75 or a choice from à la carte menu.

THE LOBSTER POT L'Etacq, tel: Jersey 82888

This restaurant is famous for its seafood and provides an excellent menu which is expensive. It is situated midway on the side of a hill and commands a marvellous view. The individual atmosphere and setting are all included in the price. £7.50 set menu. Also à la carte. Open all the year round.

MANHATTAN RESTAURANT West Centre, Bath Street, St Helier tel: Jersey 76216

A clean modern licensed restaurant serving hot spicy hamburgers American style. Expect to pay £5-£6 per head includng wine for lunch and dinner. Open all the year round.

Tea for Two

APPLE COTTAGE Rozel tel: Jersey 61002

This is a very pretty little restaurant overlooking the harbour, which is one of the most attractive on the island and very unspoilt. The 'olde worlde' cottage interior is also recommended for the excellent selection of cream teas. Prices from 90p-£1.35. Closed from November-May.

THE POTTERY RESTAURANT Gorey Village tel: Jersey 51119

This cafeteria style restaurant is open at lunchtime with a selection of dishes which include excellent sea food salads. In the afternoon fresh cream teas are also served. Examples are £4.95 for a fresh lobster salad. £2.95 crab salad. Cream teas from 75p per person. Closed at the weekends. Open all year round.

JEFFREY'S LEAP Ann Port, St Martin tel: Jersey 53339
This period style cottage is situated on a cliff edge over-looking Archirondelle Bay and is highly recommended for its cream teas. An additional attraction to the place is a legend attached to it. This was the site on which a Jersey man called Jeffrey was sentenced to death in the Middle Ages for murder. A rock on the headland nearby still marks the spot where he leapt off and fell onto the rocks below. £1.15 for scones, jam and a pot of tea. Closed October-Easter.

HOUSE OF DUPRÉ Bath Street, St Helier tel: Jersey 26046
This is a very good place to take a rest from shopping in St Helier, either during mid-morning, at lunch or teatime. It is well known Jersey department store which also has a very good country style cafe with excellent waitress service. The menu is simple and the cold buffet is moderately priced. You can either sit down to a meal or just sit and wait for a friend over a hot coffee and a sandwich. Expect to pay £4.00 for a full meal. Open all the year round during shop opening hours.

NUMBER 10 Bond Street, St Helier tel: Jersey 34400
This restaurant is good and cheap with excellent cold buffet. Lunchtime prices up to £5 per head. There is an evening menu for £4.50 not including wine. Closed Monday. Open all the year round.

Dancing

The best places for dancing during the summer are at the following nightspots:

The Regency Suite, Fort Regent, St Helier, tel; Jersey 73308
Kon Tiki, St Saviours Rd, St Helier, tel: Jersey 31021
Scarlets Discoteque, Route Dunord, tel: Jersey 61697
El Rancho, La Belle Etoile, St John, tel: Jersey 61601

Pubs

Licensing hours in Jersey are daily from 9am-11pm except Sundays when they close between 1pm and 4.30pm.

LILLIE LANGTRY La Motte Street, St Helier, tel: 26046
Named after Jersey's most famous 19th century actress the interior of this public house is crammed full of Lillie Langtry memorablia. Serves sandwiches and hot food at lunchtime.

PRINCE OF WALES TAVERN Hillgrove Street, St Helier tel: Jersey 37378
This is an old town pub, popular with the locals and it has a cosy atmosphere.

COURT HOUSE TAVERN St Brelades tel: Jersey 41510
Any local person will be able to tell you how to find this pub. It is very close to the beach and has 3 main bars and is built in a period style. It is popular and crowded out during the season. There is also a fairly pricey restaurant upstairs.

Leisure Activities

the beaches p77   walking p81   sport p88
what to see p92

Jersey has a yearly average of 1,191 hours of sunshine. To get the best of it the majority of holiday makers make a bee line for the beaches. The northern coast of Jersey exposes high cliff faces and pebbly shores. These are ideal for bathing in the morning but lose their sunlight early in the afternoon. Northern beaches tend to be pebbly, except at low or half tides, when the sandy sea bed is exposed. Tidal ranges are high. In Jersey the span is 40 feet compared with a mere 4 foot 6 inches at Brighton on the mainland, which is a considerable difference. Consequently the tide races in with great speed. Swimmers are warned to keep this in mind, especially when tempted to explore among the rocky reefs or caves.

In the south there are fewer cliffs and the sandy beaches run gradually into the sea. The gentle tilt of the sea bed enables the swimmer to wade out for some distance at high tide. At low water people often walk for miles over the wide expanses of clean yellow sand. These beaches receive the maximum rays of hot afternoon sunshine and water warms quickly. Often there are still people enjoying themselves until the sun sets which is the only reason they reluctantly decide to pack up their spades and buckets to return home.

The Beaches

BOULEY BAY Trinity

This north facing shingle beach is recommended for moderate swimmers. It is surrounded by high cliffs and hills and has a small granite jetty leading down from the quayside where there are cottages with shops and a small cafe. Bouley Hill has a steep road leading down to the jetty which was once the main route of the Grande Prix de Jersey which now no longer takes place. Now the road is prepared each Easter for an annual car rally which is a much publicised local event. Cars scream down at break neck speed and the sound of screeching car brakes fills the air for miles around. At other times the site is a favourite for go-kart and motorcycle races. The cliffs overhead are well known as a local site for hang-gliding. Finally there is a Scuba Diving School during the high season and good surfing for beginners when the sandy beach is exposed at low tide. Faces north.

ROZEL BAY St Martin

This area is surrounded by wooded cliffs and approached by roads banked by steep cötils which are hill slopes furrowed and planted by farmers according to the season. The small harbour offers safe dry anchorage for twin keeled boats and there is a selection of cottages with shops and tea room nearby. The harbour and fortifications were built as protection during the Napoleonic Wars and now

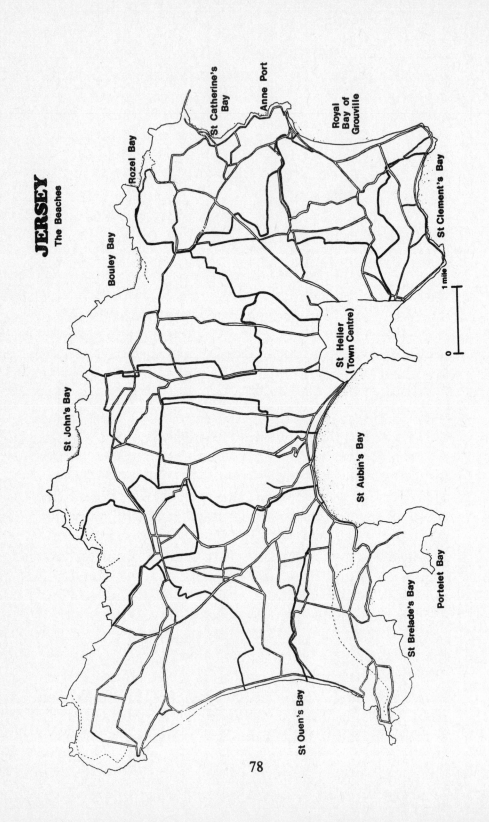

JERSEY
The Beaches

Bouley Bay

Rozel Bay

St Catherine's Bay

Anne Port

Royal Bay of Grouville

St Clement's Bay

St John's Bay

St Heller (Town Centre)

1 mile

0

St Aubin's Bay

Portelet Bay

St Brelade's Bay

St Ouen's Bay

78

offer pleasant surroundings to visit or even stay in. Faces northeast.

ST CATHERINE BAY St Martin
The breakwater sheltering this bay on the northern side was originally built as a haven for the Channel fleet during the Napoleonic Wars. After Nelson's victory at the Battle of Tragalar plans to finish building the southern arm of the harbour were abandoned. Today this mile stretch of sandy beach is pleasant and unpopulated. Faces east.

ANN PORT St Martin
This sandy beach with pebbles and a rocky shore line offers good bathing at high tide. On the headland overlooking the bay are a few cottages and wooded hills. Overlooking the beach on a cliff is Jeffrey's Leap Tea House which sells excellent cream teas. This 'tudoresque' building is the site of the medieval punishment administered to a Jersey man called Jeffrey. Faces east. (See Tea for Two).

GROUVILLE BAY Grouville
Mont Orgeuil towers over the northern side of this sandy bay which is accessible by car. Very good for non-swimmers and backed by an 18 hole golf course and Gorey Harbour which offers safe anchorage for many small vessels. There are a few shops lining the harbour. The Dolphin Pub is a well known old establishment at the harbours edge frequented by locals. Faces east.

ST CLEMENTS BAY St Clement
Surrounded by offshore reefs this beach is better for walking on at low tide than bathing. Beware of offshore tide races as ranges on the island can be as much as 40 feet and this area is known as a danger spot for people out

walking when the tide is rising in. Offshore are new mussel beds which are part of Jersey's fast growing new industry. Faces south.

ST AUBIN'S BAY St Helier

This is a major bay on the west side of St Helier which is sandy and excellent for sunbathing and attracts maximum sun. Nearby is the Old Court House public house which is popular with locals and visitors alike and stands close to the water's edge. There is a car park here and nearby is the Royal Channel Island Yacht Club. Good for a pink gin and more smart than practical. Known as the Flannel Island Yacht Club by one sailing enthusiast on the island. Faces south.

PORTELET BAY St Brelade

This sandy cove is accessible only via a steep path which runs down from the cliffs. Enclosed on three sides this sheltered spot makes a good sun trap. It is also excellent for bathing. Faces south.

ST OUENS BAY St Ouen

This is the longest beach in Jersey facing west and famous for its spectacular sunsets. Backed by sand dunes and St Ouen marsh Bird Sanctuary this beach is also a popular surfing centre where boards can be hired. It is safe for experienced swimmers only here and there are beach guards on duty during the summer. Watch out for specified 'safe swimming' flags denoting the OK areas. Cafes are dotted along the beach and are easily accessible from the coast road. Faces west.

Walking

The coast line of Jersey is magnificent. In the north craggy and precipitous cliff faces are reminiscent of a Cornish coastline. There are numerous cliff walks meandering along these rocky shores and on a clear day you can look out to a magnificent view. Each season of the year produces a particular variety of wild flora. Spring time is spectacular with burning yellow gorse and exquisite wild violets. Summertime offers clear and cloudless skies, perfect weather in which to walk and admire the island. Most parts are accessible by car and for walking it is best to park somewhere and follow the nearest footpath.

The National Trust of Jersey owns areas of land where resident and visitor alike can walk. This organisation is responsible for the preservation of land and buildings of historical importance. Property donated to the Trust or bought with money from gifts and donations of the Trust's members are then made accessible to the public. The National Trust of Jersey has no connection with it's English counterpart, but the aims are similar, particularly with regard to the preservation of land. It relys solely on donations from its members and contributions from the public. All the properties owned by the Trust are open to members and non-members alike; the properties are dotted all over the island and at the last count numbered 64. More information about the Trust can be obtained from:
The Secretary, The Elms, St Mary, Jersey, Channel Islands
Their handbook containing lists and details of all their properties is available on request.

Jersey is divided into twelve parishes, namely: St Ouen, St Mary, St John, Trinity, St Martin, Grouville, St Clement, St Saviour, St Helier, St Laurence, St Brelade and St Peter. The exact date of their formation is unknown but their names appear in records of the Middle Ages and by the end of the 12th century they were all firmly established. Each parish had a church, and the priest in each parish was designated to look after the livelihood of his parishioners. In 1331 a meeting is recorded to have taken place between the Prior of Vale in Guernsey and the Prior of St Clement in Jersey to discuss a plan to present a petition to the Privy Council demanding assistance to protect the island inhabitants against enemy onslaught. Later the responsibility assumed by the Church was replaced by island legislature drawn up by the States, but the role of the parish still plays an important part in the running of the island today.

The parish of **St Ouen** is in the north west of Jersey. Part of the coastline forms the sands of St Ouen's Bay which is the largest beach in Jersey. The sweeping sands are ideal for an evening walk and are a favourite place for many locals at sunset. The headland at L'Etacq northwards to Plémont is a famous beauty spot; one of many in Jersey. There are paths and cliffwalks leading from Les Landes Racecourse around to either side of the headland. The best way to approach this is by car, and many are found parked near Plémont or L'Etacq on a Sunday while people take some exercise after lunch. There is a ruined castle on the headland at Gronéz built across a promontory. It dates from the Middle Ages when the local inhabitants used it as a refuge in times of trouble. Le Pinacle further south was used by inhabitants on the island in Neolithic times and remains have been excavated which suggest that successive settlements existed in later centuries. Most recent archaeological discoveries are Bronze and Iron Age dwellings and a Gallo Roman temple.

St Mary is the next northern parish. Between the 14th

and 15th centuries it was one of the chief sheep farming districts on the island. The demand for wool was heavy since knitting was one of the industries depended upon by the islanders for their livelihood. La Col de la Rocque is a promontary near Devil's Hole, one of many caves scattered along the northern cliff faces. Most are accessible at low tide if you are interested in exploring them. Many were used for storing contraband in the days when privateering was commonplace. Inland at St Peters Valley is a restored Jersey farmhouse. It is the best remaining typical example of the period and dates back to 1774. Today, "the Elms", is the headquarters of the National Trust of Jersey.

The parish of **St John** begins west of Sorel point and lies between St Mary and Trinity. Views of the Paternosters and Sark can be seen from the coast on a clear day. Further south is La Route du Nord, a famous stretch of road built by the men and women of Jersey during World War II. The islanders were given this work to do by the Labour Department to provide some sort of occupation during the war; it also saved them from extreme poverty. It was originally intended to stretch as far as Sorel but was stopped suddenly at a point where it interfered with the German military zone. This is still one of the best roads on the island and easily recognisable.

On the shore below Sorel is the Fairies Bath. This is a man-made cave hollowed out of solid rock, 15' deep, and 25' x 24' wide. One explanation for its existence is that the cave was made by smugglers. Legend has it that if any man sees fairies here he will be struck blind. Further to the east are The Wolf Caves, which can be reached by boat at low tide or by a shaky rope ladder. 'La Hougue Boëte' lies inland. This megalithic tomb consists of a bowl-shaped mound and received its name from the Boiste's, an old Jersey family who came over from Normandy. Apparently it was an ancient meeting place where the Seigneur held court on the island. The district is rich in granite, and 'La Hougue Bie' is said to have been constructed from rocks lifted from St John's.

An interesting feature of this parish is the church of St John. A few years ago the vicar was surprised to find that underneath the concrete spire which was thought to be comparatively modern, lay the original granite construction which dates back hundreds of years. **Trinity** has a massive earthwork excavated by the Société Jersiaise at Le Catel. Trinity Manor in the same parish is an old manor house which is privately owned but the grounds are open to the public at certain times throughout the year. A particuarly pretty coastal area in Trinity is Rozel Harbour. The name is derived from the old Norman French word which means 'reed', indicating that this may have been a marshy area at one time. It is a well known beauty spot and a typical fishing village. The road leading to the harbour passes through valleys with côtils (steep valley faces) on one side which are used by farmers for extra agricultural land. Another place well worth visiting is the Jersey Zoo, founded by Gerald Durrell.

St Martin is the eastern parish in Jersey. The coastal area was the landing place for trading boats from Roman times. Also in this parish is Mount Orgeuil Castle, the original fortifications of which dates from the Middle Ages. At its foot, a settlement was established which soon developed into a small village. The village owes its existence primarily to the oyster beds lying offshore, which provided fishermen with an income for centuries and were declared Crown Property by the Governor in 1606. This reserved them for the Jersey fishermen who relied on them to make a living. By the 17th century this village had become a busy port which was hardly surprising as by the 1890s the industry was employing nearly 2,000 men to dredge the beds and pack up the oysters to export them to England. Competition was so fierce that at one time there were even offshore battles between the English and French over fishing rights. By the mid-19th century the industry had been killed from over-dredging but the village which remains is one of the prettiest on the island.

Southeast of Jersey is the parish of **Grouville.** The name is said to date from Roman times and is a Norman corruption of the Latin 'villa' (a farmhouse with surrounding property) and the French 'gros' (large). It seems seems that this area may have been occupied by a farm on a large estate. Lining the shoreline from St Martin to Grouville are a line of tall brick structures. These eight 'martello' towers were built during the Napoleonic wars as extra fortifications. (A similar system was used in England on the Romney marshes.) These towers were deliberately built at intervals of two gunshots so that the area of land between them could be fully covered. A favourite spot for duellists was the area between Fort Henry and Fort William when this romantic practice was in vogue. An ill-timed wager cost an army surgeon his life in 1799.

Between Grouville and St Helier is the parish of **St Saviour,** now part of the sprawling town and the site of many new office blocks and houses. Unlike St Peter Port in Guernsey, the parish of **St Helier** only developed as a busy port comparatively recently. St Brelade and Gorey were used as principal fishing villages on the island for centuries. It was only after the Newfoundland fishing boom in the early 1700s and the introduction of organised trade and a greater number of ships that a larger harbour became necessary. In 1841 Victoria Pier was built, followed shortly by Albert Pier in 1853, named after the Queen and Prince Consort. The harbour has had continuous additions ever since and is a huge commercial centre today. The best of the town can only be seen once you penetrate behind the harbour area. Many of the old place names are French in origin, such as Rouge Bouillion meaning 'red spring district', dating from the time when the mud had a reddish tint from the iron oxide in the water that ran nearby. Another road named Colomberie was an old Norman name for pidgeon house. More recent streets were named after historical events or public figures such as Waterloo, Wellington and Nelson.

Another site in St Martin is Jeffrey's Leap where according to local lore a man was accused of murder in the Middle Ages and forced to jump off the cliff edge as punishment.

La Hougue Bie is a prehistoric site with a famous legend attached. According to local lore it was widely believed that a dragon roamed the marshes between St Laurence and St Saviour terrorising the neighbourhood. It was slain by the Lord of Hambye who cut off its head and prepared to return home to celebrate his victory. His manservant, however, was so jealous of the achievement that he murdered his master and returned to court with the prized head boasting that he had killed the dragon. He also claimed that the last words his master had uttered were that he should marry the Lady of Hambye. Reluctantly she did so, only to discover the true story. Her new husband betrayed himself when he talked in his sleep. The Lady of Hambye hanged the murderer and built a chapel on the summit of La Hougue Bie which she dedicated to the soul of her dead husband. This romantic little tale is quite unsubstantiated but it is possible that in the past La Hougue Bie was known as La Hougue Hambye.

St Clement is slowly becoming absorbed into the town as more and more buildings are built in its direction. The coast is famous for walking and yachting and there is anchorage for boats in the tiny harbour.

St Laurence has an unusual set of reservoirs which have an interesting history. Waterworks Valley is a well known beauty spot which people visit year after year. At one time the stream running down the valley had enough power to turn the wheels of six water mills. Four of them are mentioned in early records as Quetevil (which was the Kings mill for grinding corn for the Crown tenants) Moulin des Ecoliers, Vicart and Petit Moulin de Le Prieur (which belonged to the Priory on L'Islet). The mills became redundant following the introduction of steam power. In 1863 an attempt was made by the Waterworks Company to make a reservoir to provide St Helier with a water supply. The present reservoirs (Millbrook, Dannermarche and Handois) are the results of work which was completed by the end of the 19th century. Today this site is owned by the National Trust of Jersey. They have recently restored one of the watermils which dates back to 1309.

According to popular belief, Waterworks Valley has a ghost of St Laurence. There is a tradition that a coach with six grey horses is driven at midnight by a coachman with white ribbons on his whip. In the carriage sits a bride dressed in white but her face is a grinning skull. Apparently, she is the ghost of a young woman of the parish who turned up at a church to be married but was abandoned before the ceremony by her bridegroom. Plunged into a state of despair, she returned home and committed suicide! But her unhappy spirit returns periodically to haunt the spot.

St Brelades is another site on the island where a small fishing village grew to be included in the town of St Helier. Now the beach is a summer holiday playground. During the 19th century **St Peter** was considered the most beautiful parish in Jersey and Queen Victoria made a point of visiting it in 1859. At one time it had the only leper house in the Channel Islands called the House of St Nicholas which was granted 40 sols a year by King John during the 13th century. There was also a small priory where two monks lived and prayed for the soul of the king and collected taxes for their mother house in Normandy. Today the parish is dominated by Jersey airport.

Westwards towards the sea is a large coastal area which has been turned into a bird sanctuary for the preservation of wild life. It occupies a large area of land to the east of St Ouen's Bay. The Trust also owns two fields called 'Le Noir Pre' and 'Le Clos du Signeur' which were brought to preserve the rare and beautiful Jersey Orchid (Orchis Laxiflora). Another property recently renovated by the Trust is an old Guard House and Magazine dating from 1765 and now restored to its original state. La Société Jersiase is another organisation which has been established to preserve sites of antiquity and archaeological interest in Jersey. They own several sites open to the public, such as the Museum in St Helier and the Hougue Bie museum. For further information contact: The Secretary, La Société Jersiaise, The Museum, Pier Road, St Helier.

Sport

Fort Regent in a vast entertainment and sports centre in St Helier where for £1.50 you can go and spend a day playing virtually any sport to your heart's content. The fortress was originally built during the Napoleonic Wars for the defence of the island but was never used for this purpose except by the Germans, occupying Jersey during the war. The States of Jersey bought it from the British Government in 1958 for only £14,500 and by 1978 had converted it into a palacial 'dream holiday' centre at a cost of 5 million pounds. Before you even begin to explore the 22 acres of tennis and squash courts, roller skating rinks and theatres you have the choice of entering by foot, escalator, or even by cable car which whisks you up from the centre of St Helier into Jersey's magnificent playground. Once inside the choice of possibilities is enormous. There are at least two late night restaurants which have dancing and entertainment. A new swimming pool, archery, badminton, basketball, karate and judo, rifle and pistol shooting, table tennis, trampolining, and even volleyball. The Leisure Centre also holds films and entertainment, conferences and trade fairs for any occasion. For further information, tel: Jersey 73000.

GOLF
There are 4 golf courses on the island:
La Moye Golf Club, St Brelade (18 holes), tel: Jersey 42701
Royal Jersey Golf Club, Grouville (18 holes), tel: Jersey 51042
Jersey Recreation Grounds, Greve d'Asszette (9 holes), tel: Jersey 21938. You can also hire golf clubs here; and
Five Mile Road, St Ouen (9 holes).

RIDING
The following stables are established centres on the island for anybody wishing to take lessons or keep themselves in training.
Bon-Air Stables, St Lawrence, tel: Jersey 63154

Broadlands Riding Centre, Broadlands, St Peter, tel: Jersey 41779

Le Claire Stables, Sunnydale, Rue Militaire, St John, tel: 62823

Sorrel Stables & Saddlery Centre, Mont Fallu, St Peter tel: 42009 (they provide tuition and livery only)

Riding is prohibited on any beach during the day between 11am-7pm between May 1st and September 30th.

TENNIS

There are courts available at Caesarean Tennis Club, Grands Vaux. tel: 22011 and at Jersey Recreation Grounds, Greve d'Azette, tel: 21938

CRICKET AND FOOTBALL

are played at the 'F.B.' playing fields at Greve d'Azette. Rugby and mini-golf can be played at Jersey Recreation Grounds.

WINDSURFING

The local windsurfing school is at Gunsite Slipway, Beaumont, tel: Jersey 42188 or 25720.

St Ouens Bay is the main place on the island for water sports. It is the longest beach in Jersey and surfing facilities are also available at:

Watersplash, St Ouen's Bay, tel: Jersey 8284, and
Sands, St Ouen's Bay, tel: Jersey 81087

Water skiing tuition is available near St Aubins Bay at La Haule, St Aubin's Bay tel: Jersey 37486 and speak to Graham McArthur. All equipment is supplied and instructions are given by qualified British Water Ski instructors. Classes are held every day from May to mid-October.

Sub aqua diving is also held at Bouley Bay. Contact:
Jersey Underwater Centre, First Tower, tel: Jersey 32813,
or
Bouley Bay, tel: Jersey 61817 and speak to Mr Webster.
Bottle filling facilities, equipment for skin diving and boat
dives are also for hire.

SAILING

St Helier is the biggest harbour in Jersey and whilst it is
more commercial than St Peter Port in Guernsey it is
expanding rapidly to accommodate the increasing number
of yachtsmen who visit the island annually. A new marina
is in the process of being built on the east side of the
harbour but there are few facilities nearby except for a
shower unless you want to walk to the shops in the town.
Most visiting yachtsmen can use either of the two sailing
clubs on the island:
The Royal Channel Islands Yacht Club, St Aubin, tel:
Jersey 41023, or
St Helier Yacht Club, South Pier, St Helier, tel: Jersey
21307
There is a Channel Island Sailing School at the High
Street in St Aubin. This is open from April-October from
9am-5pm. For details ring Jersey 63286 after 6pm.

FISHING/SEA FISHING

The best time of year to fish in Jersey is between May and
November. Pollack can be caught all the year round, but
other varieties such as mullet, bass, conger and plaice are
more likely to be found during the summer months.
Information on tides and conditions can be obtained from

Mr Smith, c/o Wheways, 16 Broad Street, St Helier, tel: Jersey 20194. He will also answer postal queries providing you send a stamped addressed envelope and an 'International Reply Paid Coupon'. There are numerous tackle shops in St Helier and also a number of Sea Angling Clubs. Jersey holds a number of records for rod caught fish among which is the record weight for the Porbeagle shark at 430 lbs. Information on tides and conditions can be obtained from most tackle shops. Harbour or pier fishing can be had from Bouley Bay, on the north coast, or eastwards from St Catherine's Breakwater. An alternative is at Bonne Nuit or Rozel Harbour, also in the north of the island. In the south, St Brelade's Bay, St Aubin's Bay, Grouville Bay, Elizabeth Castle, St Brelade's Pier and St Helier Harbour are the next best likely places.

What to See

St Helier is a busy commercial port and the centre of a thriving community. Every major store is represented here, so if you leave anything behind do not panic. The majority of French visitors spend their money at Marks and Spencer. Clothes and shoes are marginally less expensive here than elsewhere and there is also a selection of good English and Continental ranges to choose from. On the seafront Sealink and Continental passenger ferries come and go carrying hoardes of daily visitors. Statistics show that this is a popular form of arrival. The harbour is long and sprawling and there are several marinas for domestic vessels, and a new one has recently been built along the front. It takes perseverance to struggle along the Espla-

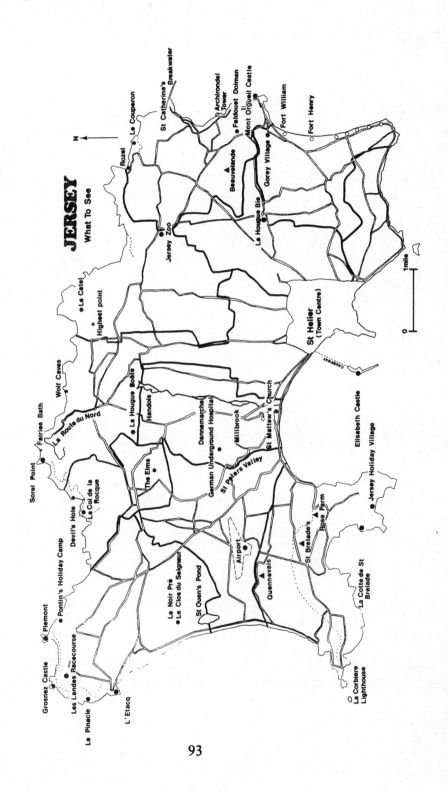

JERSEY
What To See

Sorel Point
Fairies Bath
Wolf Caves
La Route du Nord
Le Catel
Highest point
Le Couperon
Rozel
Jersey Zoo
St Catherine's
Breakwater
Archirondel Tower
Beauvelande
Faldouet Dolmen
Mont Orgueil Castle
Gorey Village
La Hougue Bie
Fort William
Fort Henry
La Hougue Boëte
Handois
Dannemarche
Millbrook
German Underground Hospital
St Mattew's Church
St Heller (Town Centre)
CAUSEWAY
Elisabeth Castle
The Elms
St Peters Valley
Jersey Holiday Village
Devil's Hole
La Col de la Rocque
Rose Farm
St Brelade's
Le Noir Pré
Le Clos du Seigneur
St Ouen's Pond
Airport
Quenneveis
La Cotte de St Brelade
Grosnez Castle
Plemont
Pontin's Holiday Camp
Les Landes Racecourse
Le Pinacle
L'Etacq
La Corbiere Lighthouse

N

0   1 mile

nade, where numerous travel firms and island tours operate, to the sedate buildings of Royal Square which stand behind.

Knowing the reputation that Jersey has quite literally earned itself from its tax haven status it is hardly surprising to find that many of the more elegant buildings in the town are banks. Every financial organisation has a name displayed somewhere on a gleaming brass plate or elegant stone carving. To the east and west stretch beaches of golden sand; the town is clean and bustling with some tall modern buildings and many signs of prestigious business enterprise. There is a competitive spirit among some of the residents on the island manifesting itself occasionally in the proud appearance of a sleek Rolls Royce. In any major city this relationship would probably pass unnoticed but in a provincial town it seems absurd.

There is a good selection of pubs and restaurants and the island is an adventure playground for any gourmet with a penchant for sea food. The choice is catholic from Italian to Chinese with chips in between. For anyone looking for variety and night life, choose the bustle of the south rather than the tranquility of the north. If you want to cook for yourself a visit to the central market in Halkett Place, under 80 tons of glass and skylight, will buy you all the food and produce you need. The famous House of Dupré store in Bath Street sells the most delicious home made chocolates you are ever likely to taste outside Harrods or Belgium. Specially wrapped in individual gold cardboard boxes, you can treat yourself or a friend to half a pound and pay approximately £2.10 pence for the extravagence. There is also an excellent cafeteria there with good waitress service selling cold salads, soups, sandwiches or coffee.

ROYAL SQUARE St Helier

The main administrative offices on the island are grouped here, which include the Royal Court House and States Chamber. This dignified square is lined with trees and in the centre stands an illustrious statue of George II. The public library is also to be found here with a rich selection of local history. The Jersey museum is only just round the corner.

JERSEY MUSEUM Pier Road, St Helier

This imposing Georgian house contains exhibits on all four floors, spanning the social and political history of Jersey from antiquity to modern times. Trace back the links between modern Jersey and Amorica, as it was once called, or browse through a rich collection of coinage and study the development of Jersey's unique banking system. The first one was established in 1797. Apparently in the 1850's many a hue and cry was raised against 'soi disant', bankers who were private individuals and who blithely issued their own bank notes. Exhibitions on display in the museum range from a 19th century reconstruction of a dental surgery to a treadmill removed from the old Jersey Prison. A stone removed from their cells still bears the inscription, carved by one unhappy prisoner in his spare moments, 'When this you see, think of me', which is sobering stuff. Another famous exhibit is the silver inlaid travelling case which belonged to Jersey born actress Lillie Langtry. On the top floor of the museum are some early aerial photographic views of the island taken during the 1930's.

ELIZABETH CASTLE L'Islet

Accessible either by foot along the causeway, or by ferry from the Esplanade at West Park during the summer. The castle was named after Queen Elizabeth I and built by the

Governor of Jersey at the time, who was Sir Walter Raleigh. The Germans added to its fortifications during the war and today there is a collection of German equipment and weaponry on display inside. Picnics are permitted within the grounds.

Open daily from March-October 9.30 - 5.30 pm. Admission. Adults 50p Children 10p.

FORT REGENT

Towering over the town this massive fortress was originally built as a defence against Napoleon between 1806 and 1814 but has never served the purpose of defending the island. A remarkable conversion completed in 1978 has transformed it into a massive sports and entertainment complex. Margot Fonteyn has danced here and each year a new selection of visiting artists are featured marking the beginning of a new summer season. All sports are catered for, squash, tennis, swimming and the admission fee includes the choice of making a spectacular entry and exit via an overhead cable car. Admission to the Aquarium, Postal and Doll Museum are free of charge. There are restaurants, and a cafeteria which surrounds the perimeter of a roller skating rink. During the season free sittings to a film called 'The Jersey Experience' are available to initiate any visitor into the historical delights of the island. The show includes vivid visual and sound effects. A visit can easily make the most of a morning or afternoon.

Admission £1.50.

JERSEY ZOO Les Augrés Manor, Trinity

A must on anybody's list of priorities if they want to see one of the world's finest zoos dedicated to the Preservation of wildlife. Founded by Gerald Durrell this zoo houses nearly 1,000 species including birds, reptiles and mammals. All are housed in superb surroundings. Special attractions are the gorillas and orangutans who amuse adults and children for hours.

Facilities include: cafeteria, shop, loos. Open all the year around except Christmas Day. Admission £1.50.

GERMAN UNDERGROUND MILITARY HOSPITAL St Laurence

A visit to this maze of underground chambers is a chilling experience. The tunnels were excavated during World War II by prisoners of war. Some are 115 feet below ground level and now contain examples of a typical wartime hospital ward, a surgical operating theatre, photographs of what went on in the islands, details of the work camps on the island and the hardships endured by prisoners under the Germans. There is a small museum attached. The underground hospital is damp and chilly. You are advised to wrap up warmly.

Facilities: car park and cafeteria. Admission Adults 85p, Children 40p.

LA HOUGUE BIE Grouville

The Hougue Bie is a megalithic passage grave that dates back over 2,000 years, and is one of the finest examples of its type surviving in western Europe. Access to the grave is through a low entrance passage which you have to bend almost double to pass through. It opens out into a large chamber. On the mound covering the grave stand 2 chapels. One was built in the Middle Ages and the second by Dean Mabon after his return from a visit to the Holy Land in 1530. The Societe Jersiase maintains the site today. There is also an agricultural museum and archaelogical collection containing examples from major sites all over the island. An old Jersey guards van stands outside which stopped running in 1929. It contains a photographic display built during the war which now contains examples of German radio equipment, medals and papers. Particularly interesting are examples of wartime efforts by the people of Jersey to produce substitutes for whatever was in short supply, like home grown tobacco for instance.

MOUNT ORGEUIL CASTLE St Martin (otherwise known as **GOREY CASTLE**)

On a clear day a climb to the summit of Gorey castle is well worth the effort. There is a magnificent view over to France on a clear day from the south east side. From the north west and north east there is a panoramic view to be seen over the island. On the way in to the castle it is possible to see the outer ramparts reinforced by Sir Walter Raleigh surrounding the original-keep which dates back to the 13th century. Inside many rooms contain wax or tableaux depicting stirring moments in the history of the castle. There is also a continuous commentary running in English and French to complement each scene presented. Open mid March – end October. 9.30-5.30 pm.

ST MATTHEWS CHURCH St Aubins Road, St Laurence

This church is unique because incorporated within the doors and the nave are some of the finest examples of art nouveau glass work designed by René Lalique. This work was commissioned in the '30's by a wealthy member of the local community. Combined with the severe stark architecture of the period the glass work looks stunning. Known locally as 'the glass church' the predominant theme is the glass angels repeated on the doors and glass screens in the nave. The windows and altar rails have a fluted design and an imposing glass cross hangs centrally about the altar.
Open Mondays-Fridays 9.00am-6.00pm; Saturdays 9.00am-3.00pm. Entrance free.

Part II
Guernsey

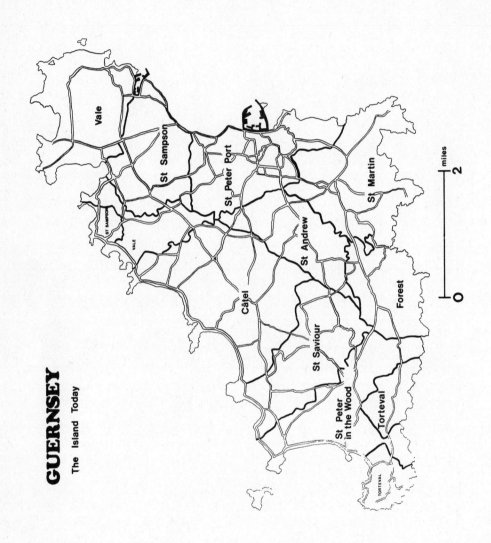

GUERNSEY
The Island Today

Vale

St Sampson

St Peter Port

St Martin

St Andrew

Câtel

St Saviour

Forest

St Peter
in the Wood

Torteval

ST SAMPSON

VALE

TORTEVAL

0   2 miles

The Island Today

Guernsey has the reputation of being the 'agricultural island'. It has numerous glass houses cultivating ripe tomatoes, which are harvested and packed for export to England. Wherever you go there are green houses to be seen parked on the edges of fields, or standing like sentinels beside a winding road. The lanes are banked on either side with high hedges or granite walls. Do not expect to find many sign posts in Guernsey as there they do not seem to know the meaning of the word. There are many maps available but a great number of visitors still get lost among the tiny lanes. Perhaps the islanders are secretly resistant to foreign visitors and would prefer to be left to their own devices. However the island attracts many visitors who are either deposited by the shipload three times daily in St Peter Port harbour or conveniently flown by plane into the awaiting airport.

Guernsey is the second largest of the Channel Islands. The main town is St Peter Port. This has the advantage of being very pretty and unspoilt, as well as being a busy commercial centre. The town houses are on a steep hill and look out on to a magnificent harbour. St Peter Port attracts many visiting yachtsmen during the summer. There is a busy shopping centre which has been made into a pedestrian precinct. Many of the houses date back to Jacobean times and line the

winding cobbled streets. A quick way to reach the top of
the hill is to climb up the high steep steps for a quick short
cut. These are to be found in several parts of the town. You
need to acquire a wandering curiosity to seek them out and
then generate enough stamina to get to the top. Once you
have done so there is a magnificent view of the harbour
from most high points and on a clear day you can see
beyond Herm and Sark to the north coast of France.

A unique feature of this town is its neatness and absence
of litter. The paths and parks are toothcombed with
refreshing regularity, which all town dwellers may know is
becoming increasingly rare. For a spectacular view climb
to the top of Victoria tower in Candie Gardens. The key is
obtainable from the fire station. Otherwise you can bring
your field glasses to the to the top of Elizabeth College or
St James' Church. Another good place for a sea view once
you have exhausted all the other possibilities is from the
balcony at Hauteville House home of the famous novelist
Victor Hugo. Many of the residential town houses are
Regency with five upstairs windows which are a cha-
racteristic of the Channel Islands. The majority of windows are shuttered which gives the cobbled streets a
distinctly French look. St Peter Port also has a fine display
of wrought iron work. It is another Regency style which
adds an English flavour to the melting pot.

During winter Guernsey assumes the sleepy character of
the other islands which is probably the time when residents
enjoy it most. During the summer, however, St Peter Port
is a crowded shopping centre and you have no need to
worry if you run out of clothes. Many visitors come from
England to sample the cheap wine and take advantage of
relaxed licensing laws. People from the Continent tend to
come for clothes. If you visit a restaurant or stay in a hotel
there is no service charge or VAT contributing to the costs.

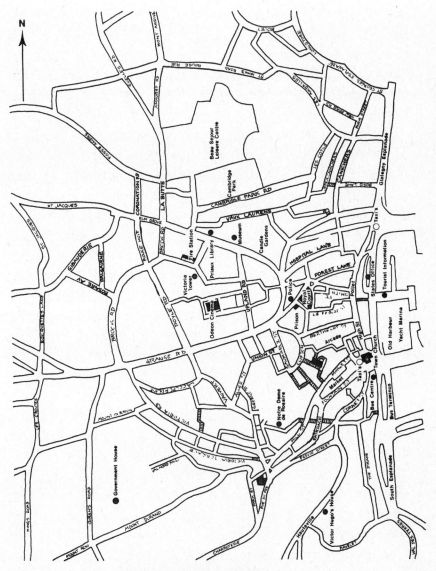

ST PETER PORT

The High Street and the Pollett are charming small lanes with shops selling continental goods which are very reasonably priced. There are many jewellery shops and an excellent market for fish and vegetables. On Thursday afternoons, in the summer, a market is held in the town centre and there are costumes and dancing with traditional goods for sale. If you want to buy yourself a Guernsey sweater, buy it here. You can also get bargains from shops which sell sailing equipment or 'seconds' from the local Thursday market. Guernseys have become a traditional feature of the Channel Islands and date from the Middle Age when the island was the centre of the stocking industry. The only shop missing is W H Smith, but there is an excellent bookshop called 'Buttons' in Smith Street for maps, tide charts and local history books. Guernseys can also be bought from:

Guernsey Knitwear, 6 The Bridge, St Sampson, Guernsey. tel: Guernsey 44487 (Guernsey's were originally knitted differently in each parish and the origin of each jersey was identifiable by the individual design).

They stock a range of parish designs from 'rope' to 'ladder'. Traditional milk cans date back to 980 AD when the French monks came over from Normandy with 'Froment du Leon', ancester of the modern Guernsey cow. You can buy these at:

Martin's Copper Shop, 2-4 The Pollett, Guernsey. tel: Guernsey 21725

They can send them to all parts of the world. These are also available from:

The Island Craft Centre, Trinity Square, St Peter Port, Guernsey.

SOME POINTS IN FAVOUR

Cheap alcohol and plenty of time to drink it in. Peaceful rural environment and helpful Tourist Committee. Pretty cobbled steets in St Peter Port with quaint little shops. Friendly people and good service.

Close to Herm and Sark for morning or day trips.

SOME POINTS AGAINST

Unreliable public transport system which changes route seasonally. Always ask for a recent copy of the bus route. The closing down of many hotels and guest houses during the winter season.

WHAT TO BRING

In winter most of the residents are distinguishable by their navy Guernseys or black PVC mackintoshes – you may even catch sight of a souwester. So you know what to bring to keep in line. In spring these are replaced by lighter clothing and a Breton beret here and there, but you will need strong wellingtons and warm clothing. In summer beachwear is a must and can be bought in the shops if you leave yours at home. Cool winds can be gusty so be prepared to wrap up.

A Short History

It seems that the Romans were as indifferent to Guernsey's natural charms as they were to those of the other islands. They left their mark – named the island Sarnia – and then a short while after, just left. There are no signs of regular Roman occupation, although the wreck of a Roman trading vessel off St Peter Port Harbour lends credibility to the theory that the Imperials used the island as a depot and half-way house for commercial voyages across the Channel.

Since they did not stay long, the Romans have left few significant signs of religious activity. There are, however, numerous examples of Pagan worship dating back to pre-Roman times in the form of standing stones and burial chambers scattered about the island. One of the oldest of these is Le Dehus Dolmen, dated between 2,500 and 3,000 BC. Arguably the most impressive is a standing stone named La Grand Mère Chimiquire, which you can find in St Martin's Churchyard. La Grand Mère is most unusual in that human features have been engraved into its surface – something rarely found in a stone of such antiquity. For more of this stone's history, see the section on Customs in

106

the Channel Islands.

Two saints are credited with bringing the Christian faith to Guernsey: Saint Maglorius and (Jersey's favourite) Hellier. Saint Maglorius, who is also known as Saint Mannelier, was probably born in Wales in the sixth century. He spent the greater part of his life in Brittany where he was ordained Bishop of Lemmeur and, later, of Dol. It was in this latter capacity that he travelled to the Channel Islands and built a monastery on Sark in 586. It is reasonable to suppose that he was also no stranger to Guernsey, for the island's Parish Church of St Sampson is dedicated to him. Guernsey's oldest surviving Christian monument is the Parish Church of The Vale and although this is dated as late as the seventh or eighth centuries, there is evidence to suggest that chapels were built and parishes established on the island as early as the fifth century. Unfortunately, none remains to be seen today.

During the 9th century the Vikings swept down from northern Europe. At first they ravaged the land, then settled in the area known as Gaul and later as Normandy. The chieftain who achieved notoriety at the time was Rollo. He established himself in northern France as a strength to be reckoned with. In 911 he signed the Treaty of St Clair sur Epte. By this Charles the Simple bestowed on him the title of Duke of Normandy. At this time the Duchy covered the Arch diocese of Rouen and the capital was Rotomagus later known as Rouen. The Channel Islands were added to the Duchy around 933. A tradition that still survives from this time is the 'Clameur de Haro' which was later instigated by Rollo to protect property and ensure fair trial between two parties engaged in any legal dispute.

WAR AND POLITICS

Apart from the gentling influence of voyaging monks, little outside interference disturbed Guernsey's island peace until Normandy officially declared a political interest in 933. The then current Duchy ruler, Duke William, made a possessive attempt to rationalise Guernsey's administrative system – under two of his own Court. On his instruction, the island was divided into two parts; from north east to south west. The Parishes of St Sampson, Andrews, Peter Port and Martin, as well as The Forest and Torteval were handed over to Neel de St Saveur, Viscount of Contentin. Anquetil, Viscount of Bessin, received those Parishes which lay to the north east of the island: Castel, St Saviour, Peter in the Wood and Vâle. Unfortunately, no one was particularly impressed by Duke William's self-imposed authority to bestow these fiefdoms upon his subjects. Following Bessin's death, Guernsey's south western Parishes were subject to 20 years of internal bickering, finally ended when Geoffrey Count of Anjou (later Henry II of England) took authority in 1137. The ancient name for this area – the Fief du Roi – dates from this time.

Say 1066 and all that, to a Channel Islander and he may look unduly pained. The Battle of Hastings was one in the eye for Harold but for the Islanders William the Conqueror's victory marked the beginning of centuries of unwanted and aggressive attention from their nearest neighbours – England and France. On William's accession, these hitherto unnoticed little spots of land suddenly acquired a political and strategic importance out of all proportion to their size: England wanted them, Normandy wanted them, and France was not indifferent. With her sister islands, Guernsey suffered the fate of a prize toy;

repeatedly snatched first by one side and then the other.

At first all was well. William of England was also Duke of Normandy and for a short while the Islanders knew security under the shadow of a powerful sovereign. But following William's death in 1087 Normandy reverted to separate rule and the battle for a Channel stepping-stone was renewed with a vengence.

Decades of cross-Channel tug-of-war games followed. During the century and a half leading up to the 100 Years' War, Jersey and Guernsey in particular were subjected to repeated invasion from both sides – and quite literally subjects to 10 separate princes. These include such historic names as William the Conqueror; England's Henrys I, II and III; John Count of Montain (King John of England from 1199; French King Phillip II and Edward I).

Not unnaturally, the people of Guernsey showed few signs of fervent loyalty to their various overseas lords at this time. King John did manage to obtain a general oath of allegiance from all the Islanders in 1206, but how far this was inspired by love and respect for a former Lord of the Islands, or by the fact that he was holding hostage members of the community of Sark, is hard to judge. It is probably fair to say that the people of Guernsey knew little and cared less about their many sovereigns (Henry III was the first ruling monarch to visit the island – and he was on his way to somewhere else); that questions of allegiance were governed not by conscience, but by self-preservation and self-interest.

The fourteenth and fifteenth centuries were times of great hardship for the Island people. During the One Hundred Years' War, from 1337 to 1443, Franco-English rivalry was at its height; island crops were burnt, cattle raided and castles provided little refuge from constant danger. An instinct for self-preservation forced the

Islanders to overcome their dislike of outside interference. They made repeated pleas for aid from both Edward I and II; for English protection from incessant French attacks on their trading vessels; and for the politically neutral status eventually granted by Papal Bull in 1483.

Meanwhile, Guernsey was acquiring an increasing degree of self-rule. By the mid-thirteenth century itinerant judges had been appointed to preside over disputes in court; wardens and bailiffs to handle more muscular matters of defence and the law. (The original Bailiff's Seal of Office sent by Edward I to Guernsey in 1279 can be seen today in the island's Greffe office.)

But the new system proved inadequate to its appointed task. Fear, tension and insecurity turned the islanders against one another; internal dissension was rife and officials open to corruption. In 1320 Guernsey Bailiff Renouf Gautier was murdered in a jealous rage by fellow official Gautier de la Salle. The spot where he stopped for absolution on the way to execution is marked today by the ancient Bailiff's Cross near St Peter Port (see Walking). Such incidents were sadly commonplace. In 1357 a Jersey man sent to aid Guernsey defend Castle Cornet from French attacks killed a prominent island official for suspected treason! Nervous Guernsey subsequently imprisoned, but later pardoned, two Jersey officials for a crime that was probably never committed. Eighteen years later, history repeated itself when Guernsey Bailiff John de Saint Martin was tried, and acquitted, twice for suspected betrayal of Gorey Castle to the enemy.

One direct result of the infighting was, predictably enough, that Guernsey society became polarised; wealth and strength protected its own, whilst the weak and disadvantaged suffered poverty and starved or maybe died. Many Guernsey residents also owned property in Normandy from the times when the island was affiliated to the Duchy, and were forced to decide which lands to protect and which to keep. The few who remained evidently acted in their best financial interests, for they later emerge as dominant names in the island's history. The leading family on Guernsey at that time was probably that of Carey – a name which you still hear on the island today.

In 1339 two other powerful families – those of York and Lancaster – involved the Islands in yet another alien conflict (Edward Earl of Rutland, later Duke of York, was warden on Guernsey at that time). In the same year, with impeccable timing, Admiral of France Sir Nicholas Béhuchet attacked and captured Guernsey and some of the lesser islands. It was 12 months before the English finally rescued the Islanders at the Battle of Stuys and a further five years before Castle Cornet was out of French hands. Sir Nicholas, however, got his just deserts and was hung from his own yardarm in proper swashbuckling style.

Guernsey has always inherited her problems – her wars – by proxy. Perhaps the most internationally controversial thing that the islanders ever did was to have a penchant for privateering; but even in this area they were never in a position to give as good as they got. It was therefore a great relief for all the Channel Islanders when they were granted neutral status in time of war by Papal Bull in 1438. Up to this point, damage to Island commerce from French attacks to their trading vessels had become so great that the French were persuaded to grant Letters of Protection for periods of up to three months. And even these were no real guarantee of safety. After 1438 however, things began to look up for the people of Guernsey; they built, traded and began to prosper. By happy coincidence the Papal Bull expired in 1689 the same year that Charles II's Order of Council forbade the import of French goods. The people of

Guernsey were now able to profit from their love of piracy and smuggling, at the same time as enjoying a home market suddenly eager for the products of indigenous trades such as knitting and cider-making.

In the early sixteenth century Civil War broke out in England and, unlike many of the other islands, Guernsey supported Parliament. This was unfortunate, for on his accession in 1668, Charles bestowed many favours on Royalist Jersey. However, all of the Islands were granted a Royal Charter and Guernsey received a new bailiff – Michael L'Epriere. L'Epriere's appointment is an interesting one in that he was the first, and only, bailiff empowered to act as a registrar at weddings.

From the seventeenth century to the twenieth, the people of Guernsey were relatively free to repair their fractured way of life. Winston Churchill visited the island in 1914, and is the first of many twentieth century statesmen to have done so. And then came the Second World War. Like the French before them; like (indeed) the English, German strategists could not believe their luck. In 1940 they invaded and took the Channel Islands.

The occupation was relatively low-key; all legal and administrative matters carried on as before, with the proviso that new rules and regulations should be submitted to the German Commandant for approval. British forces stationed on Guernsey were imprisoned, and foreign soldiers were sent to work building fortresses and bunkers, many of which still stand today. It should be said, however, that the people of Guernsey are renowed for their proud and defiant stance throughout the German Occupation. Despite threats of imprisonment or worse, some of the islanders ran an underground publication, 'GUNS', to bring much needed news and hope to their fellows. (See History of Jersey.)

After the War, life crept back to normality. In 1948 The British Nationality Act conferred special status on the Channel Islands and, in 1953, Queen Elizabeth II travelled to Guernsey. Her last visit was in 1978.

TOWNS, TOURISTS, TRADE AND TRAVEL (A SOCIAL HISTORY)

Worship and War are the two activities which have formed the social fabric of the island. Read the tourist map. You cannot take ten paces anywhere on Guernsey without catching sight of something built in praise of God or as a defence against attack.

Since medieval times, the island's community life has centred around the Church. Life was slow, hard, mainly agricultural and, above all, based on strict religious discipline. The Church was a place of authority, education, refuge, salvation, inspiration and occasionally the destination of Pilgrims. And until the Reformation in the 1550s (when the Hospital de Bosq was built), the Church was the only existing institution for the care of sick and needy islanders. During the Reformation, many religious buildings and relics were destroyed, but most of the island's churches remain as, strangely do all of its bells.

When Reformer Henry VIII was succeeded by ardent Roman Catholic 'Bloody Mary' in 1553, her alarmists cries of witch! and heretic! crossed the Channel and infected Guernsey, where many poor unfortunates were sacrificed to the general guilt and fear her fanaticism inspired. One horrific case recorded at this time was that of a mother and her two daughters who, in the process of defending themselves against a charge of stealing some pewter pots, were deemed to have given insufficient evidence of their devotion to the Roman Catholic faith. None was found guilty of theft – but all three were burnt at the stake as 'heretics'. The most tragic feature of the story is that one of the women gave birth in the fire and, although her child was rescued, it too was later thrown to the flames.

In the early seventeenth century, English kings were more concerned with political rather than religious affairs. But the accession of James II brought a new wave of Roman Catholic fervour to Guernsey. Priests were imported from the mainland, a new Roman Catholic Governor, Charles McCarthy, was appointed and Roman Catholic solidiers were even sent to garrison the castles.

But you cannot dictate what people believe; and in 1787 when John Wesley introduced the Methodist faith to Guernsey, it took a firm hold. However, between 1791 and 1793 over four thousand Roman Catholic Royalists and clergy sought sanctuary from the French Revolution on Guernsey, expanding the island's population by one-fifth and re-instating Roman Catholicism as its dominant faith.

Life on the island much have been extremely dull for these French aristocrats, accustomed as they were to the pomp and circumstance of the French Court. Social functions on Guernsey at the time were restricted to assembly room dances, tamed by the rigors of etiquette. There was little that the islanders could do to make life more interesting. In 1788 they did attempt to produce the play 'A School for Scandal', but this was considered so shocking that there were riots in St Peter Port!

The nineteenth and twentieth centuries saw a gradual easing of social and religious disciplines on the island. But Guernsey is, and will probably always remain a conservative place renowned for rustic views and well-worn pews; for historical, not social, attractions.

114

Despite the vissicitudes of war, St Peter Port grew rapidly throughout medieval times. A Parish church was built in 1048; there was an Eperquerie (building for drying fish) by 1195; work on Castle Cornet started in 1206 following England's loss of Normandy; in 1279 they built the pier; and in 1796 George III ordered that Fort George should be erected. Trade also flourished, despite French interference. St Peter Port became an important commercial centre for ships travelling between England, France and Gascony – particularly after 1689 when Charles II's boycott on imported French goods greatly increased the market value of indigenous island products such as knitwear and agricultural produce, as well as luxury goods obtained by a now flourishing privateering and smuggling trade.

The people of Guernsey are fishermen and are used to the sea, but cross-Channel trips in the sixteenth and seventeenth centuries were nothing like as easy as they are today. Then, a journey to Southampton could take as long as five days; the hazards of war and weather forced commercial sailors to travel in convoy, and even that was no guarantee of safety. Yet by the end of the seventeenth century, following a period of relative peace and prosperity gained by 100 years of neutral status, many Channel Islanders decided to seek their fortunes overseas. People from Guernsey travelled as far afield as Australia, America and New Zealand. Cambridge, Ohio, is named after Guernsey's Cambridge Park – now the site of Beau Sejour Leisure Centre. Legend has it that one of the threats, exasperated parents would offer to misbehaved offsprings was; 'I shall have you shipped to Boston'.

By the late eighteenth century island communications had begun to improve. Packet steamers carrying mail sailed regularly between Guernsey, the other islands and the mainland and in 1794 the island's first post office was instated by Act of Parliament. But the roads were appalling; sewers, if they worked at all, seeped straight into St Peter Port harbour; and the smell from the drains were so bad that the Old High Street became uninhabitable. Not surprisingly, in 1832 and 1867 the island was devasted by two virulent attacks of cholera in which 341 people died. Eventually, in 1840 work on a 'modern' sewage system was begun.

Mainland communications improved even further in 1929 with the introduction of the famous 'Flying Boat' (an early precursor of the hydrofoil) from St Peter Port to Southampton. And then in 1940, the Germans invaded and Guernsey was more isolated than she had ever been before. Radios were forbidden, petrol rationing forced the use of bicycles, and bans were applied to all social gatherings – even those of the Salvation Army!

Since the war, Guernsey has developed as an agricultural centre as well as a tourist island and attracts visitors from all over the world. It has a unique system of government and is the chief island in a Bailwick which includes Alderney and Sark. It is distinct from the other islands by its strong rustic appeal.

How to get to the Island

by air p117   by rail/sea p118   by car p120
by coach p120

By Air

The quickest way to get to Guernsey is by air. The island has a modest airport providing services to the Continent as well as main land England. International visitors are advised to fly to Jersey via Gatwick and then change flights. European visitors from Amsterdam, Paris, Cherbourg or Brussels can fly direct with KLM Airlines, Jersey European, Aurigny Air Services or Haywards Aviation. It is not necessary for visitors from the UK to present passports when entering Guernsey. But if you are intending to visit the Continent it is advisable to bring one or buy a 24 hour identity card for a short trip. These are available from ticket offices providing you remember to bring 2 passport sized photographs with you. For international visitors as well as those from the Continent the same rules of entry apply for Guernsey as for the UK. The other services which operate from the mainland are

Dan Air, British Midland, Guernsey Airlines, Brymon Airways, British Island Airways and Intra Airways. The price for a return ticket is from £64-£78 return depending on the season.

Information about current prices, flights, and timetables are available from your local travel agent. Many air lines offer reductions for advance bookings to students, for group fares or members of HM forces. Sometimes there are discounts for standby flights. Check this with the individual airline concerned as prices vary seasonally.

By Rail/Sea

British Rail operate journeys from Waterloo to Southampton and then by Sealink ferry to Guernsey.
Ordinary Adult Fares for a 3 monthly return cost £54. Most British Rail fares are generally half price for children, students or old age pensioners. The Sealink Service operates across the Channel for passengers wishing to cross by ferry. The following services are provided by British Rail and Sealink. They are economical and ideal for group or family travel. Midweek travelling is generally cheaper. Sailings are daily from May-October. Off season travel is less frequent with sometimes only four weekly so be sure to check with:
Sea Link Car Ferry Centre, 52 Grosvenor Gardens, London SW1 0AG, tel: 01-730 3440.
The following are a list of rail/sea services available to Guernsey:

CHANNEL ISLAND SEA RAIL SPECIAL A special monthly return ticket from Waterloo in any month except July and August, from Tuesdays to Thursdays only. 2nd Class cost £46.00.

8 DAY CHANNEL ISLAND BONUS HOLIDAY TICKET Available any month except July and August, from Monday to Thursday. Cost £36.00.

SEALINK NIGHTFLYER WINTER SAIL Available from Sunday to Friday from November to March. Travel begins at 11.00 pm from Waterloo, London, arriving in Guernsey at 6.00 am, allowing 6 hours before returning home at 12.00 am. Price £16.00. Good for a journey to pick up duty free liquor. For additional information contact:
Sealink Travel Ltd, Ticket and Information Office, Victoria Station; tel: 01-834 2345.

BONUS BREAKAWAYS 2 – 8 day holidays in Jersey or Guernsey inclusive of tax and insurance. The bookings can be made at either of 2 hotels providing bed and breakfast as well as dinner. Sometimes a coach tour of the island is also provided.

ANIMALS ON THE FERRY Dogs are discouraged from travelling on the ferry. Cages or kennels have to be provided by passengers without cars. Dogs may be left in the cars during the crossing at their owners risk and a cost of £7.50.

By Car

For people who want to make sure that they have transport on the island, car hire is available in Guernsey. If you want to bring your own then Sealink offer the best terms for transporting cars and their passengers to the islands. Advance booking is essential. Please remember that trailer caravans are prohibited. Dormobiles and caravans need a special certificate of authority from the States of Guernsey Tourism Committee. For Sealink bookings contact:
Sealink Car Ferries, PO Box 303, London SW1G 0AG, or Sealink UK Ltd., Weymouth Quay, Dorset, DT4 8DY, or Sealink UK Ltd., Norman House, Kettering Terrace, Portsmouth, PO2 7AE.
For further enquiries contact: 01-834 2345.

By Coach

The National Coach Service provides the cheapest form of travel to either Portsmouth or Weymouth for under £5.00. Bookings should be made in advance, or standby tickets can be obtained for as little as £2.00. Enquiries to:
The National Coach Service, Victoria Coach Station, 164 Buckingham Palace Road, London SW1. tel: 01 730-0202.

Inter-Island Travel

by air p121   by sea p122   service to the continent p122

By Air

Travelling between Guernsey, Jersey and Alderney is quicker by air though more expensive than any other form of travel. Flying to Alderney is best as sailing is restricted in summer and stops completely in winter. For flights from Guernsey to all the other islands contact:
Aurigny Air Services, The Airport. tel: Guernsey 37426; or:
Town Office, South Esplanade, St Peter Port. tel: 23474. Costs for flights between Guernsey, Alderney and Jersey are approximately £10 single. £15.00 day return. £16.00 for a 3 day return.

For flights from France contact:
Manche Voyages, J. Parmentier, 51 Boulevard Robert Schuman, Cherbourg. tel: 53-13-55, telex: 170744, cost: Single ticket £14. Return: £20.00.

By Sea

Most people staying in Guernsey enjoy a day visit to the other islands as they are so close. Condor operate a Hydrofoil service from Guernsey to Jersey, Sark and Alderney. In the summer the service is frequent. In winter only 2 sailings are scheduled every week. Travel to Alderney is restricted during the summer by sea and stops during the winter season. Contact:

Condor Passenger Department, North Pier Steps, St Peter Port, Guernsey. tel: Guernsey 26121; or their Head Office:

Sealink operate a steamer between Guernsey and Jersey every day during the summer which takes approximately $1\frac{3}{4}$ hours. Contact:

Sealink, West Centre, Bath Street, St Helier. tel: Jersey 77122.

FOR OTHER DAY TRIPS AND EXCURSIONS: from Guernsey contact:

Herm Seaway, The Esplanade, St Peter Port. tel: Guernsey 24161.

For most passenger service it is advisable to arrive at the quayside at least 20 minutes before departure to avoid missing the boat.

Services to the Continent

Condor Commodore and Shipping Services Ltd, North Pier Steps, St Peter Port, tel: Guernsey 26121 run a hydrofoil passenger service to St Malo. There are at least 4 daily sailings during the summer and this service shuts down in winter. Prices are £13.40 single, £26 return.

Condor also run a car ferry every Friday which leaves from St Peter Port to St Malo. This service continues throughout the year and prices for a 10′ car are £24.50 single, £44.20 return.

Continental people to contact for travel by sea:
Morvan Fils (Agents Generaux pour la France)
2 Place du Poids du Roi, Gare Maritime, St Malo, France, tel: St Malo 35402.
They also operate a summer service between Guernsey, Jersey, Sark and Alderney.

Travel within the Island

by car p124   by public transport p126   car hire p126
by taxi p126   motorcycles p127   by bicycle p127
by wheelchair p127, Island Tours p128

In the 19th century steam locomotion heralded the age of the train. At the end of the 19th century a Southern Railway had been built in Jersey, and Guernsey had a tram system which ran between St Peter Port and St Sampson, built in 1879 and owned by the 'Guernsey Steam Tramway Ltd'. Today it no longer exists since the arrival of the motor car quickly replaced the tram system on the island.

By Car

Today the best way to see the island is by car. If you bring your own and come via the ferry there are a few points you should know:

124

The rules of the road are similar to driving in the UK but the island limit is 5 mph slower than Jersey at 35 mph. Yellow lines are painted across the road at intersections from minor to major roads which indicate that drivers must give way. Guernsey has nearly 300 miles of winding lanes and some of these junctions are very narrow. Single yellow lines painted by the side of the road indicate no parking areas. It is an offence to stop on one, even if you remain inside the vehicle. Any accident must be reported to the police within 24 hours: The Police Station, St James' Street, St Peter Port. tel: Guernsey 25111

The speed limit on Guernsey is 35 mph.

The roads in Guernsey can be crowded in the summer. St Peter Port has a pedestrian shopping centre and a complicated one way system. Parking is limited here. There are no meters only 'parking discs'. There are adjustable clockfaces which you set at the time you leave your car. There is a parking permit depending which street you park on, that states the allotted time you may leave your vehicle unattended. Discs are obtainable from the Police Station, James Street, St Peter Port.

If you are travelling to the harbour by car it may be advisable to park outside the town and come the rest of the way by bus, because finding a space to park in, may take a long time and you may miss your boat trip. Lastly, most garages in Guernsey are closed on Sunday so remember to fill up your tank on Saturday afternoon.

For traffic and timetable enquiries on the island, tel: Guernsey 25209.

By Public Transport

There is an island bus service running in the summer. It also runs coach tours on the island. Services alter frequently. Ask at the bus centre near the station on the Esplanade:
Guernsey Railway Company Ltd, Picquet House, St Peter Port. tel: Guernsey 24677

Car Hire

All hire cars on the island have an 'H' sign on them so they are easily identifiable. Terms vary from company to company but expect to pay £8.00 per day. Conditions of hire are that you must be over 20 and under 70 years of age. Passenger liability insurance included. A clean driving licence is essential. Special terms are available off season.

By Taxi

The taxis that run in Guernsey are all licensed. Visitors arriving by ferry will find them waiting along the Esplanade or past the bus terminus near the town church. Expect to pay 50p at the start plus additional mileage.

Motorcycles

Hire cost approximately £7.50 weekly, with sidecars £15, these are available from:
H C Tostevin, Grande Rue, St Martin, Guernsey. tel: Guernsey 37671; or
Millard & Co., Victoria Road, St Peter Port, Guernsey. tel: Guernsey 21551
To hire a motorcycle you must be aged over 20 and possess a clean current driving licence or equivalent. Wearing a helmet is compulsory.

By Bicycle

Hire cost approximately £4 weekly. From:
Cycle Hire, Rue Maze, St Martins, Guernsey. tel: Guernsey 36815
Perrio Cycle Hire, Route Carre, L'Islet, St Sampson, Guernsey. tel: Guernsey 45217

By Wheelchair

If you want to hire a wheelchair or even a cot, contact:
The Hire Shop, St Peter Port. tel: Guernsey 28218. Cost for a wheelchair from £2.50 for the day to £6.25 weekly. Roofrack hire is £1.50 for a week.

Island Tours

These are run from the Bus Company near the station on the Esplanade. Contact:
Guernsey Railway Company Ltd, Picquet House, St Peter Port, tel: Guernsey 24677.

Where to Stay

hotel p130   selt catering accommodation p132
camping p136   group holiday accommodation p138

Hotels, guest houses and self-catering accommodation are all available in Guernsey. These are graded by the Island State Tourist Board to ensure that correct standards are maintained. It is possible to find accommodation easily in the winter season but for any summer holiday do book well in advance. One way of finding out what is on offer is to ask for the official booklet 'Where to Stay in Guernsey'. This is available from: States of Guernsey Tourist Committee, PO Box 23, St Peter Port, Guernsey, tel: Guernsey 24411. This office has information about local accommodation and they also run a room booking service from local hotels.

The hotels in Guernsey are divided into 2 categories. The first group are denoted by **Crowns.** The more facilities on offer, the greater the number of crowns awarded to a hotel. Expect to find a large hotel, with full liquor licence; bars open both to public and residents and a formal atmosphere. The second group are denoted by **Shields**. Expect to find a smaller hotel operating a residential drinking licence only, also a less formal atmosphere. In Guernsey the guest houses are graded between one and four **Swords.** Expect to find decent rooms with hot and cold water as well as a residential drinking licence. Other accommodation on offer may only be 'approved'. This means that it has been inspected by the Island State Tourist Board. **Approved** accommodation is up to private house or farmhouse standards. These have bathrooms and modern sanitation although they do not necessarily provide hot and cold water.

When choosing accommodation it is important to know exactly what amenities you require and whereabouts you wish to stay as well as the price range you are willing to consider paying. When booking for rooms or paying for meals there is no VAT or Service Charges in Guernsey.

Hotels

The following are a selection of hotels on the island chosen because they are all established, well known and represent a wide range of tastes. The prices given are for a single person staying half board during the low or high season. Unless specified otherwise prices given are approximate and may be subject to change.

THE ROYAL HOTEL St Peter Port, tel: Guernsey 23921, RAC, 4 Star, 4 Crown.
This large established hotel overlooks the harbour of St Peter Port and is situated on the sea front. Recommended

as a family hotel facilities include most bedrooms with private bathrooms, TVs and there is also a swimming pool. There is an extensive menu and the hotel is well known locally for having an excellent grill room. Dancing is held most nights during the high season. Prices range from £15.60-£25.00 for a single room including bed and breakfast per person per day. Open all the year round.

HOTEL HOUGUE DU POMMIER Castel, tel: Guernsey 63800
This is an early 18th century farmhouse set in a 10-acre estate. Recommended for families as well as couples, most bedrooms have private bathrooms, and a TV. There is a large car park, swimming pool, and a good restaurant which is fully licensed. The price for a single room is £14 including breakfast and an evening meal, per person per day. Open all the year round.

LE CHATEL HOTEL Fermain Bay, tel: Guernsey 35716, AA, RAC, 3 Star, 3 Crown.
This large modern hotel is built on the south east coast of Guernsey and provides a marvellous sea view which overlooks the beach. Facilities include most bedrooms with bathrooms, telephone and radio. There is a good restaurant with a continental atmosphere and the beach is easily accessible. Prices start from £16.210-£17.65 for bed, breakfast and an evening meal per person per day. Closed from October to April.

BELLVOIR FARM HOTEL Rue de la Hougue, Castel, tel: Guernsey 56004, 2 Crown.
This hotel is a converted farmhouse set in two and a half acres of land near to Vazon Bay. The rooms are all

centrally heated and most bedrooms have bathrooms en suite. This hotel has a homely atmosphere. Prices start from £10-£12.50 for bed and breakfast, per person per day.

MOORES HOTEL St Peter Port, tel: Guernsey 24452, Grade 2 Crown, AA, RAC, 2 Star.
This is a small friendly town hotel in the main town which is frequently used by locals travelling over from Alderney or Sark who need to stay overnight on the island. It is close to the shops and harbour and there is a small friendly restaurant providing English and continental dishes. Prices start at £10.35-£19.50 for bed and breakfast, per person per day. Open all the year round.

THE DUKE OF RICHMOND Cambridge Park, St Peter Port, tel: Guernsey 26221, AA, RAC, 4 Star.
This is one of Guernsey's largest hotels which overlooks St Peter Port Harbour. It is modern and new and aims to maintain high luxurious standards. There are 3 bars, a sun terrace and a private swimming pool. Prices for bed and breakfast start at £22.00-£24.00 per person per day. Open all the year round.

Self Catering Accommodation

Many people prefer self catering accommodation to staying in a hotel. For families or people holidaying 'en masse' it can often provide a cheaper alternative and often a freer more relaxed holiday. Some holiday cottages are more commercial than others; the more facilities that they have to offer, or the more luxurious and convenient obviously cost the most. Prices vary according to the season. Competition for bookings is popular and early enquiries with information regarding the number of people and dates preferred is advisable. Most approved accommodation is graded from A to C. Some arrange car hire facilities at reasonable extra cost. The following is a selection of A graded accommodation. The prices given are for the approximate cost of renting holiday accommodation weekly, during the low and high season unless specified otherwise.

ILEX LODGE Fosse Andre, St. Peter Port
Modern family flats near to the Beau Sejour Leisure Centre. Accommodation sleeps 4-6. Fully equipped kitchen, bathroom and laundry facilities. Car park, swimming pool, telephones and children's play area. Prices range from £50-£210 weekly.
Contact: Mike or Pat Sellick. tel: Guernsey 21986

VAZON BAY APARTMENTS
These apartments are tastefully designed in Guernsey granite and overlook the sandy bay. Sleeps 4-5. All facilities included. There is also a private swimming pool available for all resident guests. Prices range from £160-£260.
Contact: Rue des Goddards, Castel, Guernsey. tel: Guernsey 5433.

ST ANDREWS COURT Le Vauquedor, St Andrews, Guernsey
Modern 2 story apartments near St Peter Port. Centrally heated.
Facilities include: Colour TV, laundry and clean linen. Prices range from £72-£200 weekly, two bedroomed only.

tel: Guernsey 20107 or 24-hr answerphone 36187

VILLA THERESIA Les Adams, St Peter in the Wood, Guernsey
Choose one out of eight self contained flats in a recently converted hotel. Each sleeps up to 6 people. Central heating, colour television. Cleaning staff are available and clean linen is supplied. Swimming pool. Prices range from £75-£230 weekly.
Contact: Mr & Mrs Graham Ogier. tel: Guernsey 64018

RICHMOND COURT Vazon Bay
New well designed adjoining maisonnettes, each sleep up to 6. Consist of 2 double bedrooms, kitchen, living room, dining area, bathroom. Facilities include: laundry and telephone. Overlooks the bay. Prices range from £66-£220 weekly.
Contact: The Managing Director, L'Atlantique Hotel, Ltd. Perelle Bay, St Saviours, Guernsey. tel: 64056.

CLOS DE MER COTTAGES Grandes Rocques, Castel
Modern bungalows consisting of 2 double bedrooms, bathroom, dining room, kitchen. Facilities include: colour television. Price srange from £75-£188 weekly.
Contact: Mr Gill, 'Lone Pine', Mare de Carteret, Grandes Rocques, Guernsey. tel: Guernsey 57765

ASHMORE HOLIDAY FLATS Forest Road, St Martin
These flats are converted from a residential house set in a pleasant garden. Sleeps 4-6 people. Facilities include: colour television. Car park. No pets allowed. Prices range from £65-£160 weekly.
Contact: The Travel Centre. tel: Guernsey 35661 (Sole letting agents)

GEMINI FLATS

These flats are modern and semi detached. Near to L'Ancress and Pembroke Bays and the golf course. Each flat sleeps up to 5. Consists of 2 double bedrooms, kitchen, etc. No pets allowed. Prices range from £75-£170 weekly. Contact: Mr & Mrs Miller, L'Abri, Rue de Boullon, Vauxbelets, St Andrews. tel: Guernsey 38463

The following companies will make holiday arrangements for you:

GUERNSEY AND HERM LEISURE TRAVEL LTD

Weighbridge, Travel Centre, Lower Pollett, St Peter Port, Guernsey, tel: 21897.

They arrange holidays and inclusive terms on an individual basis.

SEA BEDS

New Jetty, St Peter Port, Guernsey, tel: Guernsey 24747

This is an accommodation service especially for people using the car ferry. Also they produce attractive brochures which show you what to expect and tell you what you are getting.

ACCOMMODATION BOOKING CENTRE

Old Mill, St Martin, Guernsey, tel: Guernsey 35661

This agency is appointed by leading airlines, Sealink and British Rail to organise their bookings. They have a choice of inclusively priced holidays.

HOLIDAY PAK LIMITED

The Travel Bureau, St Pierre du Bois, Guernsey, tel: Guernsey 64475

This company provides special adventure and package holidays. It was established in 1976 and works in conjunction with the local hotels and guest houses some airlines and Sealink. This company is run by Guernsey people and specialises in group holidays for people who wish to concentrate on: birdwatching, marine biology, angling, etc. They provide a flexible programme to suit group holidays up to 10 in number. Other services available include excursions around the island, excursions and lunches as well as the services of a guide. Finally, you can chance your luck and try this alternative for something that is a little different:

HOME INTERCHANGE LIMITED (INTERNATIONAL)
8 Hillside, High Street, Farmingham, Kent, DA4 0DD, tel; 0322 864527
This is a holiday home exchange service. It is worth contacting if this is the sort of holiday which attracts or for those of you who are flexible with a certain spirit of adventure. They do have a few members in the Channel Islands from time to time. Write or ring for information.

Camping

there are six main camping sites in Guernsey. These are all inspected and approved by the States and can offer an exciting alternative to staying in a hotel or a guest house. At any rate, prices are much cheaper and the sites listed below offer a wide range of locality to choose from. For further information contact:

Tourist Information Bureau, PO Box 23, St Peter Port, Guernsey. tel; Guernsey 23552.

THE SITES

The following are places where you can pitch a tent:

FAUXQUETS VALLEY FARM Castel, Guernsey
AA listed, families and couples preferred. Prices per night:
£1.40 adults, children under 14, 70p.
Contact: R. O. Guille. tel: Guernsey 55460

CAPELLES CAMPING CENTRE Route des Capelles, St Sampson, Guernsey Prices per night: £1.25-£1.60 adults; children under 10, 85p.
Contact: E. A. Mahy. tel: Guernsey 57468

VAUGRAT CAMPING Route de Vaugrat, St Sampsons. Prices per night: £1.50-£1.60 adults, children under 10, 80p.
Contact: J. A. Laine. tel: Guernsey 57468

L'ETOILE CAMP SITE Vale, Guernsey. Prices per night:
£1.10-£1.20 adults, children under 14, 55p.
Contact: A. M. Brache. tel: Guernsey 44325

LALEUR CAMPING SITE Torteval, Guernsey. Prices per night:
£1.10 adults, children under 14, 55p.
Contact: G. O. Robilliard. tel: Guernsey 63271

LA BAILLOTERIE Vale, Guernsey. Prices per night: 90p adults, children under 12, 50p. Closed September-Easter.
Contact: H. A. Collas. tel: Guernsey 44508

CARAVAN
Trailer caravans are not permitted in Guernsey. Motor caravans may be used as transport but more for habitation.

In any case an import licence must be obtained in advance from the States Tourist Board.

Group Holiday Accommodation

Going out with a crowd or seriously thinking of sticking to large numbers? In either case contact the following places:

Lion Table Tennis Holiday Club, Maurpas Road, St Peter Port. tel: Guernsey 38972.
This building has 4 rooms with enough beds for up to 16 people. It is recommended for family groups or large parties. There are self catering facilities for cooking, a table tennis and TV room. Rules specify that someone mut be responsible as leader for the group. Price is £5 per person for bed and breakfast daily.

Morley Methodist Youth Hostel, Fort Road, St Peter Port. tel: Guernsey 36486
Consists of a building with 2 dormitories for sleeping in. Attracts groups from schools and hostels all over Europe. Rules specify that a leader must take responsibility for the group. Prices are £35 per person weekly for bed, breakfast and evening meal, or £39 if a packed lunch is included.
The Scout Hostel, Rue Maingy, Vale. tel: Guernsey 27575
This hostel consists of 2 dormitories sleeping 12-14 in each. There is a room for leaders, kitchen and showers. Open to young people of all ages, run on usual 'hostelry' lines. Price is £1.50 per person per night.

Eating and Entertainment

restaurants p139   dancing p140

Restaurants

There are many good restaurants in Guernsey and the following are no exception. They are all in the main town and have been chosen because they are well established and open all the year round. Prices are approximate, and are for a meal per person including wine, unless stated otherwise.

OLD GOVERNMENT HOUSE HOTEL Anne's Place, St Peter Port. tel: Guernsey 24921
Provides lunch and dinner in elegant surroundings with good service. A la Carte menu or table d'hote choice. Dinner and dancing. Expensive and formal. Lunches £6.50, dinner £8.50.

THE ROYAL, ESPLANADE St Peter Port
This is a well established hotel with an extensive a la carte

menu. Excellent reputation for table side prepared food. Set menu at lunchtimes £400 not including wine. Dinner from £7.50.

STEAK AND STILTON The Quay, St Peter Port. tel: Guernsey 23921
This cellar style restaurant has a busy informal continental atmosphere and provides excellent meals. It is popular and open from lunchtime to dinner. Prices start from £8.

WHISTLERS Hauteville. tel: Guernsey 25809
This restaurant has a good local reputation for French food. Dishes are prepared from fresh produce bought at the local market. Open for lunch and dinner. Evening atmosphere is enhanced by candlelight. Dinner from £9.50.

LE BISTRO BORSALINO North Esplanade, St Peter Port. tel: Guernsey 27529
This restaurant serves very good English as well as French food and has a varied menu. There is also a Bistro Borsalino in Jersey. Lunchtime prices start from £2.75 not including wine. Dinner from £9-£10.

Dancing

A glance at the entertainment section of the *Guernsey Evening Press and Star* during the summer season will most likely give you up to date information about seasonal activities and events on the island. Most major hotels provide dinner dances. The main ones are The Royal, The Old Government House, or The Duke of Richmond.

Leisure Activities

the beaches p142   walking p147   sport p151
what to see p156   places to tempt your pocket p160

Guernsey is famous for its coastal scenery. Local claim that there are 30 bays to walk along and 34 miles of sandy beaches. Apart from the miles of southern cliff walks, the beaches on the north of the island are vast areas with rock formations formed from Guernsey Granite. Most of the houses are made with it, and in the south the colour is stone grey, turning to a rich luminous salmon on Grandes Rocques Bay.

There is a machine showing wind direction in the window of St Peter Port Tourist Office. A stroll down to the harbour to check this before you go out for a day on the beach will avoid having your picnic ruined by sand blown everywhere. The following is a list of the beaches in Guernsey.

The Beaches

L'ANCRESSE BAY Vâle
This bay is sheltered on three sides by cliffs and grassland, and is reputedly where Robert Duke of Normandy introduced Guernsey cattle. There is a small natural harbour and the sandy beach has an 18 hole golf course nearby. There is good parking close by and a restaurant at the Pembroke Hotel. Ice cream kiosks and deckchairs if you want them. Tropical Bird Aviary at L'Ancresse Lodge. Faces north.

GRAND HAVRE Vâle
This vast beach is broken up into separate sand and shingle bays and backed by a grassy common with dolmens and menhirs nearby. Very good swimming. Cafe, kiosk and loos. Faces north west.

GRANDES ROCQUES BAY Castel
Incredible shaggy rock formations with fascinating rock pools which are good for exploring. Good swimming. Cafe and restaurant nearby, deckchairs for hire and loos. Faces west.

COBO BAY Castel
Similar to Grandes Rocques in character. This is a good family beach with restricted swimming areas. Watch out for prohibited sections. Deckchairs, restaurant, icecream kiosk and loos. Faces west.

VAZON BAY Castel
One of the largest beacches on the island with maximum sunshine rate. The wide expanse of sand is sometimes used for motor racing. Good for beach games. Restricted

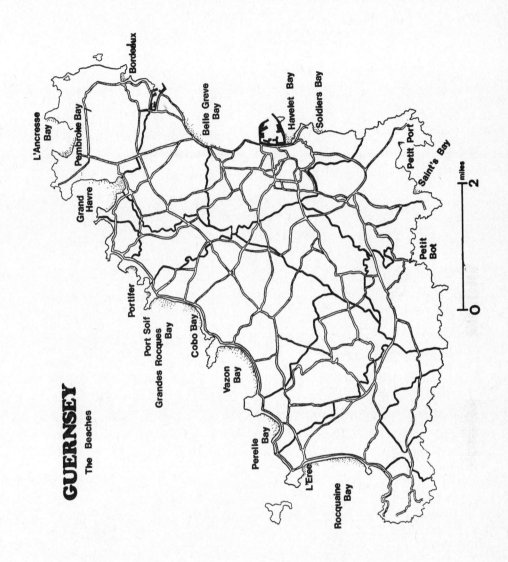

GUERNSEY

The Beaches

L'Ancresse Bay

Bordeaux

Pembroke Bay

Belle Greve Bay

Havelet Bay

Soldiers Bay

Grand Havre

Petit Port

Saint's Bay

Portifer

Petit Bot

Port Soif

Grandes Rocques Bay

Cobo Bay

Vazon Bay

Perelle Bay

L'Eree

Rocquaine Bay

miles

2

0

143

sections for bathing because of strong currents. Restaurants, cafe, icecream kiosk, hired chairs and loos. Faces west.

PORTELET BAY Torteval
Vast rocky and sandy beach. Sand and shingle surrounded by low hills and a view of Lihou Island from the shore. Excellent for bathing. Restaurant and cafe, kiosk and loos nearby. Hired deck chairs. Faces west

PETIT BOT BAY Forest
This bay is popular and pretty and accessible by car. Good for swimming. Sheltered pebbly beach with sand at low tide. Deckchairs for hire and cafe on the shore. Faces south.

MOULIN HUET BAY
Rocky atmospheric beach. There is a car park on the hill above and 100 metres of rough track leads to the shore below. Sandy areas are exposed at low tide exposing jagged rocks dividing the beach into a series of private coves. Offshore lie Dog and Lion rocks. There is a car park, cafe and loos.

FERMAIN BAY St Martin
This beautiful sandy bay is sheltered by cliffs and accessible by bus, car or boat from St Peter Port. Good for swimming. Shingle beach with sand at half tide. Restaurant and loos. Faces east.

HAVELET BAY St Peter Port
This is within walking distance of St Peter Port. Three swimming pools built out into the sea provide bathing whatever the state of the tide. There are also facilities for

water skiing or water polo in the bay. Cafe, deckchairs and loos. Faces east.

BELLE GRÈVE BAY St Sampson

East of the island and next to the coast road which runs behind the beach. Sand and shingle. Better for sunbathing than swimming. Shops, cafe and icecream kiosk. Faces east.

BORDEAUX Vâle

This small fishing harbour has interesting literary associations as it features in the novel written by Victor Hugo *Toilers of the Sea*. There is a sandy beach with scattered rocks and good swimming to be had at high tide. Cafe nearby for refreshments. Also a restaurant and icecream kiosk. Faces east.

L'EREE St Peter in the Wood

This is to be found at the northern end of Rocquaine Bay and is backed by a grassy bank. There is a cafe on the coast road providing snacks and a shop selling photographic film, magazines and beachwear. Bathing is safe whatever the state of the tide. Access is available to Lihou Island via a causeway at low tide. It is nicknamed the 'Holy Island' by locals because on it lie the remains of an old Benedictine Priory. The island is owned by Col. Patrick Wooton. Faces west.

PEMBROKE BAY Vâle

This is part of L'Ancress Bay with a golf course behind. Beautiful sandy beach. A centre for windsurfing enthusiasts. Faces north.

PERELLE BAY St Saviour

Near to Vazon Bay and providing less sand than rocks. Good for privacy and those who like to explore. Fort Richmond is within walking distance sheltered from the south by hills and trees. Faces west.

PETIT PORT St Martin

This sandy beach is on the south coast. A steep climb leads down to the beach from the cafe on the hill above. The scenery is magnificent and the place is well worth a visit if you do not mind a hike. Faces south.

PORTIFER Vâle

This is a pebbly beach and swimming is advisable between half and full tide. Also good for surfing. Faces north west.

PORT SOIF Vâle

There is excellent protection from the wind by rocks sheltering this sandy beach. Swimming is best between half and full tide. Refreshments are within walking distance at Grandes Rocques, where there is a kiosk and deckchair hire. Faces north west.

ROCQUAINE BAY

This western sandy beach is scattered with large rocks backed by low hills and some houses. The coast road runs alongside. Fort Grey and the Maritime Museum are within walking distance to the south. Northwards are Fort Saumare's and a German strongpoint. There are several cafes and also deckchairs for hire.

SAINT'S BAY

Pebbly beach exposing sand at low tide. There is a small pier for fishermen or for swimmers interested in diving. Cafe and deckchairs. Faces south.

SOLDIERS BAY
Accessible from Havelet Bay along a steep cliff path. Well worth the trek if you are looking for privacy. The water is clear and especially good for skin diving. Faces east.

Walking

Walking around Guernsey is good, cheap and fun. One advantage of being on this island is the variety of coastal scenery to be seen, and the short distance that it takes to reach it. There are still many unspoilt areas, inaccessible by car which offer a pleasant getaway if you happen to be in the wandering frame of mind. The island is divided into 10 parishes which are, Vale, St Sampson, St Peter Port, St Martin, St Andrew, Forest, Torteval, St Peter in the Wood, St Saviour and Castel.

The main town and parish of **St Peter Port** grew from a tiny village in the Middle Ages to an important port during Elizabethan times. Many of the town houses are Jacobean and the later Georgian houes date from the Newfoundland fishing boom when the islanders grew rich enough to afford an extra town house. Castle Cornet was an important fortification built during the wars raging between England and France throughout the 14th century which has had continuous additions ever since. South of St Peter Port you can walk or drive down Hauteville, past Victor Hugo's house which will lead you to countryside in a matter of minutes.

St Martin has some of the most beautiful walks in Guernsey; the whole of the south coast is famous for the jagged cliffs which stretch from Jerbourg to Pleinmont in the west of the island. Jerbourg is said to have once been the site of an ancient castle. Offshore are the 'Peastacks' called Le Petit Aiguillon, Le Gros Aiguillon and L'Aiguillon d'Andrelot which were revered by passing seamen for many centuries. They used to remove their hats or even throw an offering into the sea when they sailed past. Westwards, Icart Point is a well-known spot to stand and gaze east or west for fine views of coastline stretching either side of it. Victor Hugo used to visit the place often and even built a house there called 'La Villette' which he used as a country retreat when he needed a change of scene.

The parish of **Forest** was one of the chief agricultural areas on the island during the 19th century although today much of the parish is covered by the island airport. La Moye Point still has the relics of a Napoleonic battery built as an island defence and this is another point from which to obtain a spectacular sea view.

St Peter in the Wood and **Torteval** lie to the south west of Guernsey. The "Creux Mahie" is a tiny creek which contains one of the largest caves on the island. It is 200' long and the entrance is between 40' and 20' wide. Fishermen used to use it for storing nets and lobster pots and built huge fires which illuminated the coastline for passing ships, hundreds of years ago.

The coastline on the west coast of Guernsey has a completely different character to the rest of the island. The land levels out to rocky bays and sweeping sandy beaches which make the north west coast popular with swimmers in the Summer. Years ago, the sites which look so innocent today told a different story. Past Fort Grey which is now a Maritime Museum is Lihou Island. In the Middle Ages the site had a monastery where the monks are reputed to have practised black magic. During the 14th century a murder was committed there by an islander who was slain by the current Bailiff, Ranulf Gautier. Gautier de la Salle imprisoned the so-called sorcerer in Castle Cornet where, out of jealousy, he murdered him. Eventually the Bailiff was found out and sentenced to death, and the site where he stopped for absolution on the way to the gallows is immortalised as Bailiffs Cross near St Peter Port.

North of Lihou is a site called Le Catioroc. This was well-known as a place where witches held their covens, and the Trepied Dolmen that stands there was attributed with magical powers for the part that it played in their illegal ceremonies. Witchcraft is believed to have been widely practised in Guernsey; the last case was tried in St Peter Port in 1912. A local witch was accused by a French woman of casting a spell on her and attempting blackmail. Apparently she had originally approached this witch who was well known on the island, to cure her cattle of a mysterious disease. She was given a powder and instructed to bury it in her garden at the four points of the compass. During the trial, these treasures were unearthed and revealed to be baking powder. Since there was insufficient evidence the Guernsey court was unable to impose a serious sentence on the witch and eventually imprisoned her for 8 days for disorderly conduct.

Northwards towards **St Saviours** the beaches become extremely rocky. The granite for which Guernsey is famous gradually turn from a dull grey to a magnificent shade of copper. At sunset, the rocks glow with a curious irridiscence which could almost be termed 'post-cardy'. Through **Castel** the rocky formations taper and spread out along the shore where the land assumes the smooth quality of plains and grassland. Here in the **Vâle** there are dunes and offshore rocks and next to Grande Havre Bay is the site of an old racecourse.

St Sampson to the south has a small fishing harbour which is built of grey granite and grew from a small village to a major yachting centre. Before arriving back at St Peter Port, there is a large commercial area which you can't fail to see, where the Guernsey tomato crops are packaged and exported annually. The 1,000 acres of glasshouses on the island produce a total of 50,000 tons of tomatoes.

St Andrew is the central parish in Guernsey and the only one without any coastline. Instead of visiting the beach you can spend a pleasant afternoon wandering along the numerous lanes and roads on foot or by car.

The National Trust of Guernsey is responsible for the preservation of land and many buildings of historical interest on the island. The Trust owns approximately 32 properties divided into 12 large areas. These are well looked after and many of the walks have seats placed at vantage points where the best views can be enjoyed. The Guernsey National Trust is an entirely separate body from it's English counterpart and relies on gifts and legacies or the subscriptions of its members for financial assistance. It is possible for members of the Guernsey National Trust to enter the English National Trust properties at a reduced rate. Contact the Public Relations Office for any further information:

Mrs le Pelley, Courtil de L'Eglise, Rohais, Guernsey, Channel Islands.

Sport

RIDING

There are various riding schools in Guernsey and show jumping events, a summer show and a Horse of the Year Show that takes place annually. For information and dates contact:

Mrs Count, Secretary, Guernsey Show Jumping Association, Takapuna, Park Lane, St Peter Port, Guernsey. tel: Guernsey 20338

Other places to contact for riding:

Guernsey Equestrian & Saddlery Centre, Les Grandes Capelles, St Sampson, Guernsey. tel: Guernsey 25257. Cost: £3-5.00 per hour.

West Riding & Trekking Centre, Le Desert Farm, Les Callettes, St Saviour's. tel: Guernsey 63719. Cost: approx. £3.00 per hour.

Manor Riding Stables, Les Camps, St Martins, Guernsey. tel: Guernsey 38275. Cost: from £2.50 per hour for group lessons.

GOLF

The Royal Guernsey Golf Club, L'Ancresse Common, Vale. tel: Guernsey 46523 is north of the island. Temporary membership is available for visitors already belonging to a regular club. This one is an 18 hole course...

SQUASH

Apart from the Beau Sejour Leisure Centre, the King's Leisure Centre, King's Road, St Peter Port is available for regular players.
Contact: Guernsey 23366

Also there is the Squash Racquets Association. Ring or write to: The Secretary, La Boutefeve, Blanche pierre Lane, St Martins. tel: Guernsey 36874.

BADMINTON

The Badminton Association, Lynton, Grand Rue, Vale, Guernsey. tel: Guernsey 46048. There are also courts for hire at Badminton Hall, Rohais, St Peter Port.

ATHLETICS

Bridge Park, St Peter Port

SHOOTING

Guernsey Rifle Club, Les Fontenelles, Mount Herman, St Peter Port. tel: Guernsey 2095

THE BEAU SEJOUR LEISURE CENTRE

Modern, multi purpose, and magnificent, you name it and they play it in this vast new leisure centre in the middle of Cambridge Park. Best way is to list the activities: swimming, sauna, solarium, shops, cafeteria, concerts, theatre, bowls, netball, tennis, badminton, softball, trampoline, weight training, roller skating, roller disco, chess, dodgems, 'astroglide'.

Entrance charges: Adults 20p; Children 15p with additional charges on admission.

Contact: For recorded information tel: Guernsey 28555. For bookings, tel: Guernsey 26964. For reception, tel: Guernsey 27211

WINDSURFING

There is an International Windsurfing School in Guernsey run by Peter Vivian who was British Sailboard Champion in 1979. It is situated at Cobo Bay on the west coast. Guernsey is considered to be one of the finest windsurfing venues in northern Europe. There is a large area of shallow water protected by reefs. One week courses in windsurfing are held. The package includes: certificates in windsurfing, travel, and 7 nights basic accommodation, rental charges for wet suits and boards, utilisation of a land simulator, transfers from hotel and beach, and departure to the airport if applicable, plus tuition, starts from around £200 or £5 per hour.

Contact: GCS Travel Ltd, 41 St Georges Esplanade, St Peter Port, Guernsey. tel: Guernsey 21460; or ring: Guernsey 57417 and ask for Pete.

SAILING

St Peter Port is the biggest harbour in Guernsey available for the yachtsman. The marina is 72 acres in area and there is also the Old Harbour and Albert Dock marina for visiting craft. Recommended times are April, May, June and September. The marina is accessible 3 hours either side of high water. Anyone arriving from the Continent must have a passport and no animals are allowed other than from the Channel Islands or the UK. Frequency of St Peter Port radio is 2381/kc/s.

Facilities include: loos and hot water on the quay. There are restaurants, laundry and chandlery firms, banking and car hire available in the town. Fuel is available from the castle emplacement.

Contact: States Harbour Master. tel: Guernsey 20229
Marina Office, tel: Guernsey 25987

YACHT CHARTERING

Visitors exploring the several islands should consider chartering a yacht, rather than staying in different hotels. From between £300-400 per week, costs for an experienced sailing family can work out cheaper than in a hotel. Guernsey Yacht Chartering Ltd. hire out skippered or self sail vessels and are members of the Yacht Charter Association. Reliable advice on requirements and suitability of vessels is available. Also you can have individual sailing tuition from qualified instructors.

Contact: Guernsey Yacht Chartering Ltd., Alderney House, Grand Bouet, St Peter Port, tel: Guernsey 22357 Boats for charter, sail or power, self sail or skippered.

There are two clubs on the island offering hospitality to visiting yachtsmen. The Guernsey Sailing Club and the Royal Channel Islands Yacht Club both offer temporary membership for the use of their facilities. Anyone interested in crewing or taking part in the many racing events which take place around the island, should contact the secretary at either of these clubs:

Guernsey Sailing Club, Castle Emplacement, St Peter Port, Guernsey. tel: Guernsey 22838

Royal Channel Islands Yacht Club, Victoria Pier, St Peter Port.

SURFING

The best beaches recommended for surfing by the British Surfing Association are the following:

DOM HUE: $5\frac{1}{2}$ miles west of St Peter port. The Beach faces NW. There is good surfing all the year round and conditions are best in spring and autumn. Not suitable for beginners.

VAZON BAY: 4 miles west of St Peter Port. The beach

also faces NW. Surfing all the year round and best in spring and autumn.

WATER SKIING
The Horseshoe Ski School, Havelet Bay
Contact: 3 George Place, Union Street, St Peter Port. tel: Guernsey 23350/28083

SUB AQUA
Blue Dolphin Sub Aqua Club
Contact: Les Gemeaux, Rue des Cottes, St Sampsons. tel: Guernsey 53878

FISHING/SEA FISHING
There are no rivers but excellent sea fishing to be had around St Peter Port Harbour. Round the south coast and near to St Sampson congers are caught to make the local dish conger soup. Ormers are another delicacy obtainable from the sea which are shell fish. Local waters hold mullet, mackerel, turbot, wrasse and bass. Further off shore you could bump into sharks and dog fish. One way to get away to sea is to get friendly with a local fisherman. Another is to contact:
MV Island Fisher, Trident Kiosk, Weighbridge, St Peter Port who organise fishing trips.

GUERNSEY SEA ANGLERS CLUB President Mr Ernie Baker
Contact: Bakers, 43 The Pollet, St Peter Port. tel: Guernsey 21139

Guernsey are proud of holding 12 current British records for rod caught fish. Over 70 species have been caught. Guernsey has a maximum tidal rate of 30-40 feet in spring tides. Great care must be taken when fishing off the rocky islets as with a rising rate of 30 feet in 6 hours the weather can catch up on you if you are not careful. Good places for rod fishing are:

Fort Doyle or Jerbourg Point which are popular for garfish, pollack, mackerel and grey mullet, St Peter Port and St Sampsons Harbour for pollack, bass, bream, mullet, wrasse.

Bait: Fresh sandeels and mackerel can be bought from the local market. A mixture can be bought from the market in St Peter Port. Ragworms or lugworms can be dug up on the beaches. Frozen sandeels and squid from tackle shops. There are many places to buy equipment in St Peter Port apart from Baker's and the following offer an alternative:

Tackle and Accessories Centre, 30 Bordage, St Peter Port. tel: Guernsey 23225

G. Domaille, The Bridge, St Sampsons. tel: Guernsey 44542

Marquand Brothers Ltd, North Quay, St Peter Port. tel: Guernsey 20962

What to See

ROYAL COURT COURT ROW

For anyone interested in how the islands are run a visit to this unique parliament at the top of Smith Street is essential. There are no political parties in the Channel Islands. Their system of law dates back to Norman times and is based on ancient Norman fuedal law. The granite faced buildings date from 1799. The States meet on the last Wednesday of every month except in August. Visit the public gallery and witness the formalities of voting in French.

GUERNSEY

What To See

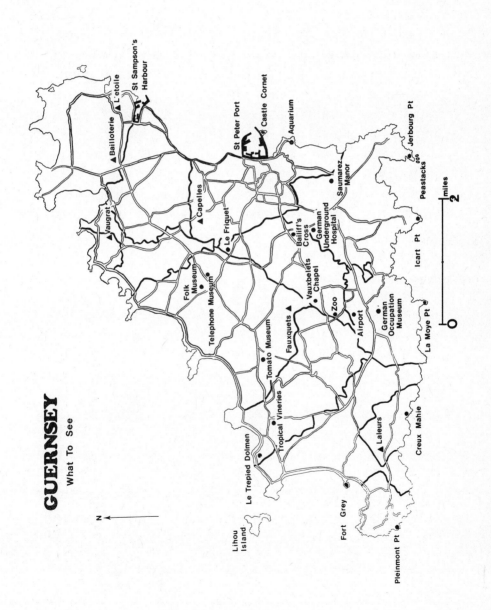

157

HAUTEVILLE HOUSE

Guernsey people are immensely proud of anyone famous connected with the islands. Victor Hugo lived on the islands from 1855 – 1870 and wrote a novel dedicated to the people of Guernsey called *Toilers of the Sea*. During his time of exile from France he divided his time between renovating Hauteville House and his literary work. The house stands as a monument to this extraordinary man. It was entirely redecorated with heavy oak carvings, tapestries and Dutch ceramics. There are many features of innovation which mark Victor Hugo as a master of design. Each room is fantastic and peculiar. Some contain examples of his own painting and carving and personal memorabilia are to be seen everywhere. The house is owned and run by the City of Paris and there is a compulsory guided tour.

Admission: Adults 40. Children 20p. Closed Sundays and Thursday afternoon.

GUERNSEY MUSEUM & ART GALLERY Candie Gardens

This award winning museum was opened in 1978. The art gallery has a variety of exhibitions which change at intervals, and a permanent exhibition of local island watercolours. The museum has a bright modern interior and exhibits the history of Guernsey and the other islands of the Bailiwick from prehistoric to modern times. Pushbutton technology set slide shows in motion depicting local natural history. You can stay for a free film in the next door auditorium which seats about forty people. There is a good bookstall for local history. Outside, the bandstand has been converted into a tea room where you can read and munch a cake in peace. Open all the year around from 10.30-4.30 pm. March-October until 5.30 pm.

Admission: Adults 50p. Children 20p.

PRIAULX LIBRARY Candie Gardens
Situated behind the museum this old fashioned public library is perfect for a rainy day. Row upon row of leather bound books harbour a mine of information. This library houses the most comprehensive collection of books on local history. Ask for Miss Cook who will offer endless patience and advice on any volume you may be looking for. Watch out for Victor Coyshe a well known paragon of historical research.

NOTRE DAME DU ROSAIRE CHURCH Burnt Lane
This Roman Catholic church with a ceiling resembling an upturned boat. Services on a Sunday are conducted by the Canon, Pere Maurice Lecuze in a mixture of Latin and French. Aspiring French musicians play here during the summer. Best to look in the local paper for details.
Services: Sunday 9.30 am and 10.30 am, and 5.30 pm, Saturday 5.30 pm.
Holydays 9.00 am, 11.00 am and 5.30 pm.

TOWN CHURCH High Street
Reputedly the finest church in Guernsey this one dates back to Norman times. The chancel is 12th century, the chapel is 15th and inscriptions on the floor are in French.

CASTLE CORNET Harbour
Castle Cornet is an impressive sight to visitors coming by sea. At night the castle is lit up. During the day it contains an impressive array of armour on show to visitors. The causeway leading to the castle is recommended by locals who buy fresh shellfish there. There is also a good fishing spot from the lighthouse platform.

THE AQUARIUM Havelet

An escape from the heat of the midday sun or from an occasional rainy day into the Aquarium is an interesting prospect. The site is a tunnel excavated into rock which was originally intended to run as a tramway from St Peter Port to Saints Bay. Now this cavern displays luminous tanks containing live examples of local and tropical fish, such as lion and coral or sea horse and conger.

Places to Tempt your Pocket

GUERNSEY POTTERY Petite Capelles Road

Here you can walk round and see the various stages of pottery production from, throwing to decorating, glazing and firing. In the workshops you can talk to the experts, who can tell you anything you need to know about one of the world's oldest crafts. An attractive shop sells ashtrays, mugs, bowls, salt holders, plant hanging pots and a selection of practical items. The results of this particular industry all have a distinctive majolica glaze. Next door there is an excellent restaurant run by local staff, which provides good country dishes cafeteria style. Coffee is served all day. Lunch is from 12.00 and there is tea served mid-afternoon.

Open all the year round. Mon-Sat 10.00 am-5.00 pm. Open on Sundays from April-September.

LE FRIQUET FLOWER & BUTTERFLY CENTRE Le Friquet Road, Castel

The centre consists of an impressive array of green houses. Further inspection reveals row upon row of carnations,

chrysanthemums, roses and other flowers, all in various stages of production. A special attraction is the Butterfly House where a varied selection of these exotic creatures roam and breed freely. Try to distinguish between the European and tropical species. There is a cafe alongside serving cakes and tea. Nearby you can also play a round of mini golf or crazy croquet. An ornamental pond on one side of the lawn doubles as a display area for sailing model warships.
Open April-September 10.00 am-6.00 pm.

GUERNSEY TOMATO MUSEUM King's Mills, Castel
There would be a gap in your education if you came to Guernsey without visiting this privately run concern to find out about the most thriving industry on the island. Did you know that when tomatoes were first introduced to Guernsey markets in 1863 that they were thought to be poisonous? For this, another enlightening gems of information about the vegetable industry in general, do visit the museum. Wander through glass houses and the galaxy of tomatoes which you can see, smell, touch and even drink in the adjoining cafe. There is also an optional sound track at the push of a button for the visitor who wants additional information.
Open Easter – October 10.00 am-5.30 pm. Admission: Adults 60p. Children 30p.

NATIONAL TRUST OF GUERNSEY FOLK MUSEUM Saumarez Park, Catel
The old Manor House is now used as a nursing home for elderly people. The stables have been converted to house a fascinating collection of old Guernsey museum pieces. Many of the more senior visitors from Guernsey will remember travelling in some of the horsedrawn vehicles on

display outside in the courtyard. Inside the buildings are tableaux of a traditional Guernsey kitchen and bedroom. Upstairs in a newly converted loft are examples of a rare horsedrawn plough and various farming implements. All the displays are rearranged annually and voluntary staff look after the building under the watchful and capable eye of Mrs Carey.

Open daily April-October from 10.00-12.30 am and 2.00-5.30 pm.

Admission: Adults 40p. Children 20p.

LES VAUXBELETS St Andrew

This little chapel has earned a place in the Guiness Book of Records as the smallest Roman Catholic church in the world. It was built singlehanded by Brother Deodat of the Brothers of the Christian School Order in 1923. This tiny monument is a dazzling example of one man's resourcefulness and imagination. The only materials available to the priest were broken pieces of glass and china, and ormershells which are studded all over the interior and exterior of the Church, neatly set into the concrete. Inside there is also a tiny altar and room for a priest and a congregation of two. On a sunny day this intricate structure is transformed into a glittering grotto.

Open daily all the year around.

SAUMAREZ MANOR St Martins

This is one of the few manor houses on the island open to the public. The house was erected in Norman times and has been subjected to numerous alternations. The additions are evidence of Tudor, Queen Anne, Regency and Victorian architecture. The de Saumarez family is one of the oldest in the Channel Islands and dates back to 1254. The house changed hands in the 16th century due to the absence of an heir and returned to the family again in the 18 century.

Open May-September on Wednesdays, Thursdays and Bank Holidays 10-00-12.00 am and 2.30-5.00 pm.

Admission: Adults 50p and Children 20p

GERMAN OCCUPATION MUSEUM Les Housards, Forest

This is a private collection of German relics from the Occupation. It has been on display to the public since 1966 and is the largest in the Channel Islands. There are displays of German uniform and weaponry and examples of transport. A typical bunker room and occupation kitchen are two tableaux on display.

Open May-mid October. 10.00-12.30 am and 1.30-5.30 pm.

Open all day in August.

GERMAN MILITARY UNDERGROUND HOSPITAL La Vassalerie

This was first opened to the public in 1954. Today this vast empty chamber is remarkable if one considers the conditions which existed when it was built. Some 60,000 tons of solid rock were excavated over a period of $3\frac{1}{2}$ years by the Todt workforce during the Occupation. This has left a skeletal area that cover 75,000 sq feet which consists of $1\frac{1}{4}$ miles of rooms and corridors.

Open daily from 10.00-12.00 am and 2.00-5.00 pm.

GUERNSEY ZOO St Andrew's

This is a small children's zoo run by two people. You can see llamas, pelicans, a flamingo pool and visit an open aviary. One aim of the zoo is to help endangered species and it welcomes your support. Children delight in the minature donkey and pony.

Open daily from 10.00-12.00 am and 2.00-5.00 pm daily.

FORT GREY MARITIME MUSEUM Rocquaine Bay

This museum is appropriately within sight of the treacherous reefs responsible for many of the ships wrecked on Hanois Reef before the lighthouse was built. Today the fort has been restored by the Ancient Monuments Committee and houses many relics. It is accessible via a causeway.

Open daily from May-October 10.00-12.30 am and 2.00-5.30 pm

Admission: Adults 40p. Children 20p.

TROPICAL VINERIES Les Rouvets, Perelle, St Saviour

Have you ever been through a banana walk or pineapple plantation? If not, here is your opportunity to find out what it is like. Coffee and tea are cultivated here where an oasis and a desert exist almost side by side. There is a small tea garden.

Open 10.00 am-5.00 pm all the year around.

HANGING STRAWBERRY FARM Les Issues, St Saviour

These strawberries are unusually cultivated in hanging vines. they can be picked to eat on the premises or taken home. At the same time you can visit the children's playground, visit the woodcarvers shop or play a round of crazy golf before having tea. There are barbeques on selected evenings throughout the summer with a country and western band. Pony trekking is also arranged from the farm. Facilities: car park and loos.

Open daily from 10.00 am-6.00 pm. tel: Guernsey 64428

TELEPHONE MUSEUM Cobo Road, Castel

This is a private collection of telephones from their earliest date of use in Guernsey in 1898 to the present day.

Open Tuesday and Thursday 7.00pm—11.00pm. Summer only.

GUILLES-ALLÉS MUSEUM and LIBRARY Market Street, St Peter Port
If you feel the urge to borrow a book you can do so at the library, providing you pay a small subscription. This library was once used as Assembly rooms and has recently undergone extensive renovation.
Open Monday-Saturday, 9.30 am-5.30 pm. Closed on Thursday.

COACH HOUSE GALLERY Les Islets, Guernsey
For anyone interested in contemporary arts and crafts with either a view to collecting, or simply to learn more about current artists and their work, then a visit to this gallery will be well worth your while. It was started in 1975 in premises converted from an old farmhouse and outbuildings. The work exhibited inside covers a wide range of media which includes painting, printmaking, photography, ceramics, glass and weaving. For an original and imaginative gift prices start at around £10 and progress upwards. Serious work is considerably more expensive.

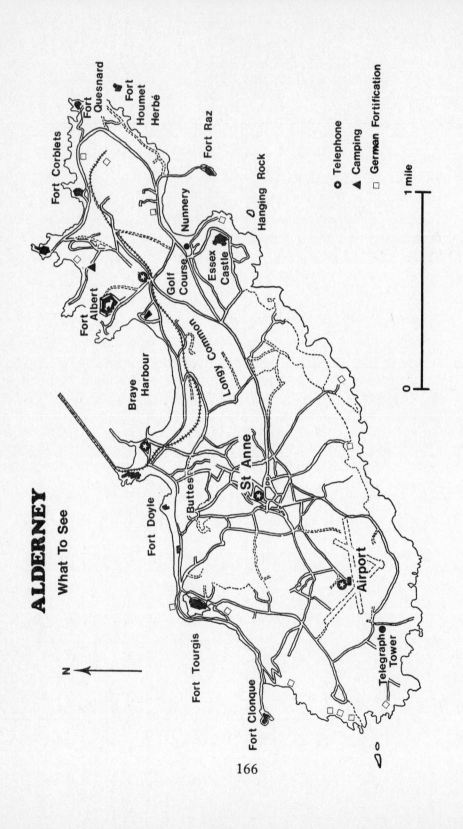

ALDERNEY

What To See

N

Fort Corblets

Fort Quesnard

Fort Houmet Herbé

Fort Raz

Nunnery

Hanging Rock

Fort Albert

Golf Course

Essex Castle

Braye Harbour

Longy Common

Buttes

St Anne

Fort Doyle

Airport

Fort Tourgis

Telegraph Tower

Fort Clonque

○ Telephone

▲ Camping

□ German Fortification

0   1 mile

Part III
Alderney

The Island Today

For an island which is modest in size compared to neighbouring Guernsey, Alderney has earned itself a considerable reputation. It survived an enemy occupation during the war and the face of the island bears scars from this period in its history. People are still drawn to the island fascinated by details of the past and eager to discover what really went on there. Many are struck by the evidence that still remains to be seen on Alderney of its wartime experience. The island is pitted with concrete bunkers at every strategic point, though most are overgrown with prickly gorse bushes. These remainders of the past now have a use as picnic spots or as adventure playgrounds for unsuspecting children. They are also good vantage points for any walker eager for a good sea view but for visitors with more than a passing knowledge of Alderney history, these edifices evoke strong emotions. These are relics from a period never likely to be forgotten.

The island is some 3 miles long and has a maximum breadth of 1 mile. The physical appearance of the island is rugged. It has steep cliffs surrounding the north west side and is permanently windswept. Leaving the west coast there are quiet coves, and a few wide beaches. An approach made from the air is spectacular in the tiny orange tri-lander which seats up to 12 people. A flight on one of these may be the nearest you will ever get to fulfilling any ambition you may have to fly your own private jet. From the air the island looks barren and sparse in winter. There are few trees and the town of St Annes spreads out from the central part of the island. Much of Alderney is covered in gorse. This glows in spring and the island is well known for the mass of wild flowers which burst forth each summer. A feature of Alderney is the friendliness of the people who live there. It is renowned for the warmth of its community. Walk into any pub and you will immediately be welcomed and accepted as part of the scene. The social life of the island revolves around the pubs, which may be few in number but have generous licensing hours. Everybody congregates there and alcohol is consumed in large quantities.

All the residents in Alderney now are English speaking. The evacuation during the war disrupted community life and now there are few residents who can trace their ancestry back to before the war. Exploration in the pubs will reap rewards if you are at all interested in island history. You may bump into seasoned local islanders like Richard Simonet for instance, who is not only the finest stonemason on the island but also far too modest to admit it.

A visit to Alderney is necessary for anybody interested in walking. The headland is magnificent and winds sweep across the island. Passionate geologists will find heaven here. Alderney is famous for a rich variety of minerals and stones. Alderney has an elusive charm. This is self evident judging from the varying opinions of visitors who stay on the island. Research also shows that no one leaves without making a firm decision that the island is either marvellous or dreadful. The same windswept landscape which appears ugly to some presents a mysterious beauty and challenge to others. If this is to be your first visit to Alderney, buy your ticket, and treat yourself to a friendly game of Russian Roulette. The chances are that you will have a wonderful time.

SOME POINTS IN FAVOUR

The warm friendly community which revolves around pub life. Extended drinking hours with enough time to pick up all the island gossip whilst having a quick pint. A variety of walks and bracing sea air.

SOME POINTS AGAINST

Minimum sea service from Guernsey to Alderney.

WHAT TO BRING

You can buy most essentials on the island but you will have a problem buying extra clothes. Better check your packing carefully unless you feel happy spending the entire holiday wearing a fisherman's outfit. Bring air sick pills if you don't like flying — be sure to take one before climbing on the tri-lander. The approach to the island has strong air currents which blow these tiny planes about on a windy day.

A Short History

Alderney history can be traced back thousands of years. Archaeologists have discovered that stone age man survived here. When Alderney was still part of the mainland Continent it provided good hunting ground. Nomadic hunters came in pursuit of game or fish and to gather food. Remains of these activities and a few flints have been unearthed, but no other physical remains of early man survive. The formation of glaciers and changes in sea level shaped the island as we know it today. It lay uninhabited for thousands of years during the ice age. The next clue that we have pointing to island settlers are the megalithic burial chambers which date from Neolithic times. There are similar examples to be seen in Brittany which range from pasage graves opening out into large chambers (such as La Hougue Bie in Jersey) to small 'cists' or individual graves. Rock a L'Epine above Fort Tourgis is a small cist in Alderney.

The island had a variety of megalithic sites which were dismantled by workers in the 19th century searching for a rich supply of granite to build walls and fortifications. The building of German fortifications obliterated other Neolithic sites. Bronze implements from 800 BC have been found on Longy Common, which are now housed in

Guernsey Museum. Pottery has also been excavated at Les Hugettes that dates from 100 BC. This was a working area as indicated by the primitive fires used for firing clay pots. Human remains were also cremated here, thus during this time Alderney must have had a sizeable community living on the island. No sign of these dwellings remains today, since they were probably built from local timber.

During Roman times Alderney was referred to as Riduna. The island developed as a trading station between Gaul, England and Ireland. An early Roman site which remains to be seen is known as 'the Nunnery' near Longy Bay, which dates from the 3rd century AD. Remains have also been discovered of another early trading station nearby on Essex Hill, built nearly 100 years later. According to local legend St Vignalis was responsible for converting Alderney to Christianity around 575 AD, and after the fall of the Roman Empire Christianity had already become an established religion. The early church adopted the administrative provinces that had already been introduced by the Romans. Alderney was included in the Bishoprick of Coutances which was formerly known as Coutancia. The conversion of the island meant that many of the old pagan beliefs and popular ancient rituals were incorporated into the old religion. Several holy sites were built deliberately to replace the old, and one example of this is at Mannez, which is near several pagan burial sites. The largest stream on the island, now near to Rose Farms at Les Rocquettes, was another ancient site.

Before Duke William conquered England, Alderney was granted to the Monastery of Mont St Michel, some 20 years earlier. This was to compensate for the loss of the north east half of Guernsey by the Abbey in 1042. The Abbey was then given Noirmont in Jersey instead of Alderney in 1057. By then the island was under the domain of the Bishop of Coutances and Duke William, who by 1066 was King of England. This link with the Crown formed the basis of a relationship and loyalty to the Crown which has been a feature of the Channel Islands ever since. The strength of this allegiance became apparent after the loss of the islands in 1204 by King John to the French. Alderney remained loyal to England despite open attacks from the French. One half of the island was run by the Bishop of Coutances, and a document, drawn up in 1236, outlined the rights of the inhabitants. One of the earliest windmills recorded in western Europe existed on Alderney. The local watermill was owned by the Bishop and milled the island wheat, which could be used by the islanders in return for a proportion of milled wheat which they paid instead of taxes. They depended on sheep farming and fishing for their livelihood. Island officers were appointed to run the administration of the island, to ensure that dues were paid, and maintain payment of the King's revenue from a population of around 300.

In 1337 King Edward III declared war on France, this war was to span a century. Alderney was captured by the French in 1338 and was not relieved by the English until the following year. These invasions were to continue throughout the next 100 years. Eventually a Papal Bull of Neutrality was issued by Pope Sixtus IV after appeals by islanders and a request by Edward IV in 1483. All the Channel Islands were declared neutral in times of war between France and England. Inhabitants on the island at this time were mostly descended from the old Norman families, as well as some who had settled from elsewhere. Le Cocques, Simons, Botts, and Gaudioins were all Breton in origin. The town centre was surrounded by walls and hedges and most houses were supplied with water from wells. The population at this time numbered 700 and

Longy harbour was the main jetty on the island. Today you can still see the remains at low tide.

The wars that raged between England and France affected the island economy. Without trading concessions arranged with the Continent which enabled trade to continue periodically with France, the situation would have been unendurable. By the reign of Henry VIII piracy had become established in the Channel. In 1549 the French had succeeded in over running Sark. The English were alarmed to such an extent that the construction of a Fort was planned above Longy Harbour in an attempt to provide a naval refuge from the French, as well as a vantage point from which to concentrate English attacks. The death of Henry VIII and the short reign of Edward VI left operations in the hands of Queen Mary. The island had largely escaped the effect of the Reformation but since the policies in England were drastically changed the project for building extra fortifications was also abandoned in 1553. Fort Essex was later built on the same site.

Huguenot refugees fleeing from France settled in Alderney in the early part of the reign of Queen Elizabeth I. Their presence owes such to the foundation of the Presbyterian religion. Names like Odouaire, Bareuson, Batise and Renier are all island names which can be traced back to the Huguenots. By 1568 the Channel Islands no longer remained under the Diocese of Coutances. They formed part of the new See of Winchester which is still a diocese today. During the reign of Elizabeth the building of fortfications were also undertaken on the island, under the direction of Sir Walter Raleigh who was then Governor of the Channel Islands.

Essex Castle was built in Alderney, which although built during the reign of Elizabeth I was named much later and does not owe its name to the Earl of Essex executed for treason in 1601. Much of the building work was supervised by Marshall Trubeville, who was bitterly resented by the islanders and who was recalled to England, after a petition of complaints against him had been presented to the Privy Council. Sir Leonard Chamberlain was Governor of Jersey at the time and had some influence over Alderney. His son, John, paid £20 and £13.6.8d. annually to rent it in 1584. The population on Alderney at this time was about 700. A contract was drawn up in 1585 clearly stating his right as Lord of the Manor, but the Council was not prepared for the unrest and discord among the islanders as a result. It was imperative that they remained united to defend the island against possible invasion.

The Earl of Essex bought the island and rights for £1000 in 1591 but there is no record that he ever made any visit there. After his execution in 1601 his rights passed to William Chamberlain. It seems that the younger brother of John Chamberlain was just as open to abuse. The islanders complained that Chamberlain deprived the island of its Minister, by failing to provide adequate payments for him to work, and that he quite openly seized far more than his fair share of the island revenue. His possessions were defined by the Royal Commissioners of Guernsey, who ordered him to pay enough to maintain a Minister on the island, which amounted to an annual salary of £20. Eventually the Church Assembly appointed Simon Masson in 1607, who remained Minister until 1652. The Chamberlain family held the lease of the island until the outbreak of Civil War. Alderney and Guernsey were then held by parliamentary forces when the Lieutenant Governor of Alderney was a Captain Nicholas Ling. After the restoration of Charles II in 1660 all former rights to the island were cancelled and the island was granted to the Carteret family, who were strong Jersey royalists. The rights of island ownership were granted to George Carteret for an annual rent of 13s.

New Jersey was given to the Carteret family by Charles II at his Restoration and the poorer islanders were encouraged to emigrate to America. An Ordinance was enforced by the Alderney Court to make sure the island had no more dependents. In 1682 Sir Edmund Andros bought the rights of Alderney from Sir George Carteret's widow. He later became the Governor of New York and passed on his power over the island to Thomas Le Mesurier, who lived in St Peter in the Wood, Guernsey. The island was later divided in a fued between Le Mesurier and Thomas Le Cocq, the local judge who attacked the newly appointed governor for being a Guernseyman. However the Le Mesurier family was to control the island throughout the 18th century when the island was undergoing its greatest period of expansion. Braye Harbour was completed in 1736 to replace the old Longy Harbour, plans which were carried through by Le Mesurier. He was later succeeded as Governor by his younger brother John Le Mesurier.

By the mid 18th century many of the islanders were engaged in privateering. The legal plundering of enemy vessels proved far more profitable than farming. A booming trade smuggling illegal alcohol developed, alongside the legitimate breeding and export of Alderney cattle. It was during this period, under the auspices of the Le Mesurier family, that the town of St Anne grew to the size we know it today. Government House, the Church Clock Tower and the first Court House were built and by the end of 1781 an island militia had been assembled. Town houses were built, and further expansion occurred at the outset of the French Revolution when 300 soldiers were garrisoned on the island in barracks by the Nunnery, and Fort Doyle was built. Methodism was introduced to the island by John Wesley. The Divers Inn in Braye Street is the original site where he preached in 1787.

At the end of the Napoleonic wars troops were withdrawn from the island and peacetime measures were introduced. Smuggling was banned which encouraged it even more. Prosperity on Alderney ground to a halt and plans for new buildings were abandoned. General Le Mesurier was soon writing to the government for funds to relieve his embarrassing financial predicament. Eventually he surrendered his grant to the island in 1825 and retired to Poole in Dorset. The property he built was called Alderney Manor and is now a housing estate. All the adjoining roads are taken from names of the islands such as Alderney or Herm Road.

Common land in Alderney was divided among the local community in 1830. This provided a suitable form of income to the impoverished 1,000 or more surviving islanders. The strengthening of French defences at Cherbourg alarmed the English government to such an extent that measures were again taken to improve the defences of Alderney in 1844. Braye Harbour underwent considerable changes. A breakwater and a chain of Forts was built which stretched from the south east tip of the island where Fort Essex stood along the coast to Fort Clonque. These operations increased the prosperity of the island since labourers were imported especially to undertake the building work. By 1861 the population is recorded to have reached nearly 5,000. The Irish potatoe famine brought large numbers of families from Ireland. An entirely new street was built, as well as a Court House and a prison. After a visit by Queen Victoria and Prince Albert in 1854 the Rue de Grosnez was named after her.

An important industry which developed in Alderney was the quarrying of the local granite. By World War I one fifth of the local population were earning a living from the local quarry at Braye. Fishing and agriculture came a close second. By 1843 Alderney had opened a post office and as communications improved the possibilities of tourism became apparent. An airport was opened in 1935 which was the first in the Channel Islands. On June 23rd 1940 the majority of the islanders were evacuated from Alderney by the Royal Navy and moved to Great Britain. This was the result of much deliberation, and when the arrival of German forces became inevitable there was little time left to transport valuables or possessions and orders were given that the maximum personal allowance was one suitcase per person. Livestock and domestic animals were let loose, and those unable to fend for themselves were humanely slaughtered. As little as possible was left for the Germans to use to their advantage. Livestock were let loose on the airport runway, all firearms locked away and the island radio system smashed. Only seven people refused to move, and so were left on the island when the Germans invaded on 30th June 1940. Conditions on Alderney during the occupation, as on all of the islands, were grim. The island was manned by German soldiers, and emphasis was given to the building of heavy fortifications, many of which remain today. This work was undertaken by an imported labour force consisting of Russians, Spanish, and later French prisoners of war. The purpose of the Todt workers, as they were called, was to build these fortifications and perform any other manual work on the island. Alderney had no concentration camp, but the workers put in over 12 hours hard labour a day, and were expected to survive on inadequate food rations which consisted of thin tea, watery soup and bread. The hardship endured was enormous, many died and were buried in mass graves now covered by the green turf of Longy Common. At the end of the war the islanders returned to an Alderney that was greatly changed from the one they had left six years earlier.

Many were to return to homes that no longer existed. Even if the buildings remained, most were gutted. Between the time the islanders had left their homes, and the arrival of the German forces the buildings were looted, at least that is what the Germans reported. No one admitted that boats had been sighted travelling between Alderney and Guernsey. Considering that conditions for such a journey were normally thought too dangerous there must have been a very good reason for them to travel. The liberation of Alderney by the army led to more goods being misappropriated.

Whatever the reason, islanders returning to their homes, and issued with government furniture in the absence of their own, noted these facts with dismay. Finally, a decision was made that the remaining furniture should be collected together and issued at random to those in need. The rest was auctioned off. This situation proved most unsatisfactory, and occasions arose for a long time afterwards when the favourite chair, for instance, belonging to one neighbour was seen conspicously displayed in someone else's house. Naturally this situation caused problems. The administration organised by the Home Office ended in 1948. Agriculture was re-established, land re-surveyed, and legislation drawn up regarding house purchase. There was no insurance for damage inflicted to property during the war years, and although the Governmment offered some financial aid most people had to manage as best they could. Many other changes occurred; the island community had entirely changed, and the administration was required to alter with it.

How to get to the Island

by air p180   by sea 181

Alderney is not easily accessible. Visitors from England must first travel to Guernsey or Jersey. During the summer there is a sea service run by Condor but this shuts down in winter and then the island is only approachable by the tiny tri-lander planes operated by Aurigny Air Services.

By Air

This is the quickest way to get to Alderney. Passengers flying from England usually have to change flights in Guernsey or Jersey.

AURIGNY AIR SERVICES run frequent flights to Alderney throughout the year and have daily, weekend or weekly return fllights available. A return ticket from Guernsey costs about £15 and day returns are slightly cheaper than an ordinary single. Aurigny also provides flights from

Southampton, Guernsey and Jersey and run 3 flights weekly from Southampton, Bournemouth and Shoreham. Contact: Aurigny Air Services, High Street, St Annes, Alderney. tel: Alderney 2609; or
Aurigny Air Services, South Esplanade, Guernsey, St Peter Port. tel: Alderney 37426; or
Aurigny Air Services, Weighbridge, St Helier, Jersey. tel: 35733
One other alternative is to contact:
Alderney Air Ferries Ltd., PO Box 3, Alderney, Channel Islands. tel: Alderney 2993/2129
A return flight from Bournemouth costs £37.00 return. Day returns from £23.90 and single flights £18.50.

By Sea

During summer the island is approachable by hydrofoil from either Guernsey or Jersey. (See Inter-Island Travel.)

Inter-Island Travel

By Sea

CONDOR HYDROFOILS LIMITED offers day trips to Alderney from Guernsey (45 minutes) and Jersey ($2\frac{1}{2}$ hours via Guernsey and Sark).
Contact: JERSEY Commodore Shipping Services Ltd., 28 Conway Street, Jersey; or Albert Quay, St Helier, Jersey. tel: Jersey 36331
GUERNSEY Commodore Shipping Services Ltd., North Pier Steps, St Peter Port, Guernsey. tel: Guernsey 26121.

Travel within the Island

by rail p183   by car p183   by car hire p184
by taxi p185   by bicycle p185   by public transport p185
island tours p186

By Rail

The Alderney Railway opened in 1847 and is the only one still in operation in the islands. Today it only runs in the summer, for adults and children to enjoy a short run from Braye Harbour to Corbeleos Bay.

By Car

It is not possible for visitors to bring their own cars to Alderney. There is a cargo boat which operates occasionally from Guernsey for people who want to move house or intend staying on the island for some time. In most cases it is easier to use the car hire facilities available on the island.

There are lots of cars to be seen on Alderney but these are all in varying states of repair since there is no MOT on the island. The smartest cars to be seen are usually the one hired by visitors and these are distinguishable by an 'H' number plate on the back.

Car Hire

To hire any car on Alderney a clean current British driving licence is essential. Some international licences are also valid. Car hire and petrol is available from:

ALDERNEY MOTORS Marais Square, St Anne. tel: Alderney 2138

MOURIAUX MOTORS Viront, Les Mouriaux. tel: Alderney 2476

RIDUNA GARAGE Ferndale Estate. tel: 2919

ALDERNEY STORES AND BUNKERING CO. LTD., Braye. tel: Alderney 2682

By Taxi

For a tour of the island, or a way of transporting your baggage from A to B, a call to the following establishments, could provide you with the travel you are asking for. Expect to pay 50p at the start plus additional mileage.

ALDERNEY TAXI'S INC. tel: 2992/2611
BELLE VUE TAXIS tel: 2658

Bicycle

Alderney is so small, that the best way to get around is by bicycle. Remember if you are planning an island tour – start by bicycling ANTI clockwise around Alderney and most of your ride will be pleasantly, downhill. Bicycles available from:

J.B. BICYCLE HIRE Olivier Street, Alderney. tel: 2294/2267 from Easter – end September.

Public Transport

There is a bus service operating on the island during the summer which operates between the main beaches and St Annes.

Island Tours

VICTORIA PRIVATE HOTEL Victoria Street, St Anes, tel: 2754

Organise daily tours of the island either by car or by mini bus depending on numbers throughout the season.

Where to Stay

hotels p187   self catering accommodation p190
camping p192   caravans p192

There is no official accommodation service in Alderney. There is an accommodation list which is available on request from Alderney Tourism Committee, St Anne, Alderney. tel: Alderney 2811. There are about two dozen hotels and guest houses on the island as well as additional self catering accommodation. There is no grading system in operation on the island.

Hotels

The following list of hotels offer a range of different types of accommodation according to your needs. The prices given are for a single person staying daily at half board. Prices are approximate and may be subject to change.

BELLE VUE HOTEL Buttes Road, The Buttes, Alderney. tel: 2844

This hotel is family run, open all the year round, except holidays over Christmas and New Year. Near to Buttes playing fields on the outskirts of St Anne and within walking distance of Saline Bay. Prices start from £11.80 per person for bed, breakfast, and evening meal. Closed for Christmas, and New Year.

HOTEL CHEZ ANDRE Victoria Steet, Alderney. tel: 2777/2788
Open all year. Definitely at the upper end of the market this hotel is comfortable and uncommercialised. Situated on the cobble streets of St Anne there are two bars in this hotel and a restaurant which has an excellent reputation among the locals. Some bedrooms have private bathrooms and a television. All have hot and cold water. Prices start from £12 per person for bed and breakfast to £16.75 plus evening meal. Closed end October–Easter.

HARBOUR LIGHTS HOTEL Newtown. tel: 2168
Simple family hotel near Braye Bay. Bar is open to non-residents. There is also a games room and some bedrooms are in a separate annexe in the grounds. Ideal for visiting yachtsmen. Prices are £10.50 per person for bed and breakfast to £15.00 plus evening meal. Closed October–Easter.

THE VICTORIA HOTEL 1 Victoria Street. tel: 2754
This is a small, medium priced hotel in St Anne's main street not far from Braye Beach. Hot and cold water in all rooms, sauna baths and a TV lounge. Prices are £9.50 per person for bed, breakfast and evening meal. Closed for Christmas.

BUTES LODGE HOTEL Butes Road. tel: 2844/2199
BTA recommended, and open all the year round except

over Christmas. This little hotel has a quiet atmosphere. There is a bar/lounge and a restaurant open to non-residents. This hotel is not suitable for children under 5. Prices are £11.80 per person for bed, breakfast and evening meal. Closed over Christmas and New Year.

THE TOWN HOUSE High Street, Alderney. tel: 2571; Management: 2330
Central to St Annes. A family style, comfortable hotel. Open all the year round. Hot and cold water. Television room, bed and breakfast. Evening meal extra if required. Not suitable for children under 10. Only £8 per person for bed and breakfast – £11.00 plus evening meal. Closed over Christmas and New Year.

THE ROYAL CONNAUGHT HOTEL Connaught Square, St Annes. tel: 2756
Small hotel in the centre of St Annes. Set in an elegant Georgian Square. Well known and recommended for seafood, and salad in the bar. Dining room is candle lit in the evening, and patio lunches are also available during the summer. Hot and cold water, early morning tea making facilities, some rooms with private baths and there are two which have large four poster beds. Prices start at £12 for bed and breakfast to £14.40 per person for evening meal included.

DEVEREUX COUNTRY HOUSE Longy Bay. tel: 2549
Seven minutes away from Longy Beach, and adjacent to a golf course. There is hot and cold water, a residents bar, a games room and a small kitchen. Prices start at £14.00 per person for bed, breakfast and evening meal.

ROSE AND CROWN HOTEL Le Huret. tel: 2600
This is a small comfortable hotel near to the High Street in St Annes. Hot and cold water, bed and breakfast terms are also available. Bar also serves cold food and snacks. Price for a single room per person is £6.25, plus breakfast is £7.25. Closed October-May.

THE GEORGIAN HOUSE HOTEL Victoria Street, Alderney. tel: 2471
This is another hotel in the town centre, well modernised, with a television in each bedroom. Hot and cold water also available. Prices start at £10 per person for bed and breakfast, to £16.00 plus evening meal. Closed during Christmas week.

Self Catering Accommodation

The following estate agents manage a wide range of self catering accommodation all the year round:

C. BELL & CO. LTD. 2 Victoria Street, Alderney. tel: Alderney 2562

M. PHILLIPS & CO. LTD. 39 High Street, Alderney. tel: Alderney 3110

BURHOU ISLAND
It may be that you have always wanted to experience staying on a tiny island overnight, alone. Even if you have not it may surprise you to learn that such an experience is available to you for a modest price of £1. Burhou Island is uninhabited except for the birds that nest there, and lies

two miles north of Braye Harbour. A rebuilt stone hut is the only rentable accommodation. There is no drinking water on the island, and no official landing place. No dogs are permitted and the island is only approachable by sea and on a calm day. Good Luck! Applications to:
The Clerk of States, States Office, Alderney, for bookings.

FORT CLONQUE South West Alderney

The idea of staying in a Napoleonic Fortress separated from land by 300 yards of causeway and approachable only on foot, depending on the state of the tides, is an exciting prospect. If it sounds what you are looking for then you may enjoy staying in this unusual setting. The Fort was purchased by the Landmark Trust in 1966. The aim of the charity is the preservation of historic and important buildings by letting them out to visitors who will appreciate their historical value and also help pay towards the upkeep of the building at the same time. Fort Clonque was refortified by the German occupying forces in 1940. It is small by military standards and has a commanding view of Burhou Island and beyond to the Casquets. It has been converted and is now suitable for a maximum party of nine and has seven single and two bunk beds. There is also a bath and a shower, cooking and heating are run on gas. An open fire can be lit if required. Linen is not provided and a caretaker is employed to look after this property. Well behaved dogs are allowed but no cats. For bookings and enquiries contact:
The Landmark Trust, Shottesbrooke, near Maidenhead, Berks. tel: Littlewick Green 3431. Prices start at £154 rising to £238. During 3 January-27 March the price per person staying at the Fort is only £9 plus £25 booking fee.

Camping

There is only one site on the island where camping is permitted, which is at Saye Bay on the north east coast of Alderney. Camping equipment is not provided and other facilities, such as water and WC arrangements, must be made with Mr Carré at Saye Farm. However the freedom that this kind of site allows is perfecct if you want to enjoy a cheap holiday and love being out of doors. Transistors are not permitted. The cost of camping at Saye Farm is only £1 weekly. Enquiries to:
Mr Carré, Saye Farm, Alderney. tel: Alderney 2196
Some camping facilities are available from:
The Sail Loft, Braye Steet, St Annes. tel: Alderney 2278

Caravans

No caravans are permitted on Alderney.

Eating and Entertainment

restaurants p193   pubs p195

Restaurants

THE OLD BARN Longis Bay, tel: 2537
This restaurant is run by Maurice Kutner. He used to be head chef of the Chez Andre and before that he worked at the Dorchester. Continental sea food is a speciality. Closed Mondays. Open the rest of the week until 11.00 pm. Good value. Open only in the evening. Prices are from £10.

THE FIRST AND LAST Braye Street, tel 3162
This restaurant is well known for the good quality of its food and locals go here to get good value for money. Seafood is a speciality. Open only in the evening. Examples for lunch are fish with chips for £2.50. Half a lobster for dinner costs, £6.50, wine not included.

CHEZ ANDRE HOTEL Queen Victoria Street. tel: Alderney 2848

Open April-October. Serves an excellent cold buffet lunch or home made sandwiches. Also dinners until 11.00 pm and a special hot lunch on Sundays for £3.75 per person. Friendly local atmosphere, à la carte menu at dinner. Prices from £9-£10 per person.

THE ALBERT HOUSE INN Queen Victoria Street, tel: Alderney 2243
This serves lunch and dinner and is fairly expensive. You can pay £6.00 for a cold lunch. Crab/lobster dinners cost £10-£12.

THE GEORGIAN Victoria Street, St Anne. tel: Alderney 2471
Recommended for food and open all the year round. Snack lunches and salads are a speciality. £6.00 for dinner.

LE COURIER Victoria Street. tel: Alderney 2869
Cafe and a tearoom for morning coffee, lunch and afternoon cup of tea. Doubles as a restaurant at night with a choice of English or Italian food. £5 for dinner not including wine.

MERMAID RESTAURANT Braye Street, tel: Alderney 3197
Open only in the summer. Serves lunch and dinner. The ground floor serves take-away. Downstairs crab and seafood specialties. Lunches cost from 55p-£4.25. Dinner can cost from £2.50 for plaice, fish or steak not including wine to £6.00 for a 3 course dinner. Closed October-March.

Pubs

Spirits are cheaper in Alderney than on the mainland and measures are more generous. Many bars provide good food or snacks and lunches. Licensing hours on the island are from 10.00 am-1.00 pm and 8.00 pm-2.00 am Monday to Saturday. Hours of Sunday are from 12.00 am-2.00 pm and 8.00 pm-2.00 am. These are the main island pubs:

CHEZ ANDRE HOTEL Queen Victoria Street. tel: Alderney 2777
Open April-October. Good meals, lunch and supper up to 11.00 pm. Special hot lunch served on Sundays. Popular local pub and very willing staff. Home made sandwiches and drinks to order.

DIVERS INN Braye
John Wesley spent the night here in 1777. This pub is near the harbour and always crowded with locals, which is a good sign.

CORONATION INN 36 High Street
A particularly good place to go and pick up local gossip. The people who go regularly have great allegiance to this pub.

ALBERT HOUSE INN Queen Victoria Street
Recently taken over in March 1981 by David Wright, who has retired from the navy. Serves sandwiches and food.

ALDERNEY SAILING CLUB Braye Harbour
This is a yachtsman's drinking club and popular with locals. Visitors and members of other recognised yacht clubs are welcome.

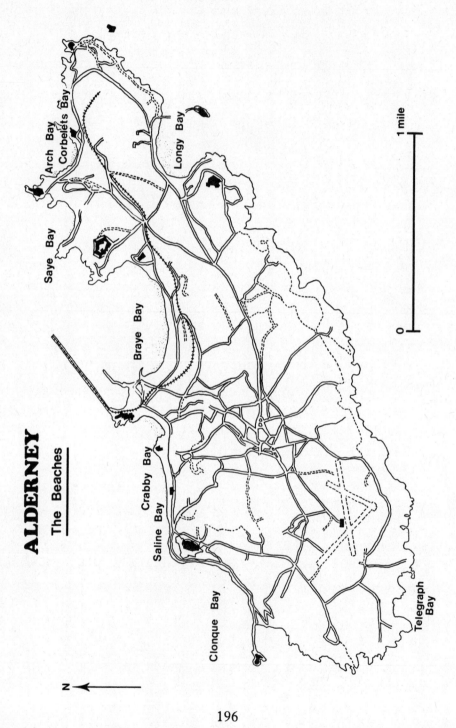

ALDERNEY

The Beaches

Saye Bay

Arch Bay

Corbelets Bay

Longy Bay

Braye Bay

Crabby Bay

Saline Bay

Clonque Bay

Telegraph Bay

N

0   1 mile

Leisure Activities

the beaches p197   what to see p200   sport p197

The beaches of Alderney are clean and unspoilt. During the summer public transport is available to some beaches and operates from St Annes. Check the wind directions before you go to avoid being blown away.

The Beaches

BRAYE BAY
This is Alderney's largest beach on the north east of the island and only a few minutes away from St Annes. Low tide reveals a long white stretch of sand. Bathing here is ideal at all times. This is the only beach which has an ice-cream kiosk and sometimes there is a drinks van during the summer. Faces north.

SAYE BAY
The locals pronounce this 'Soy' Bay. East of Braye this beautiful sandy cove is well sheltered and ideal for small

children. Bathing here is safe at all times. Faces north.

ARCH & CORBELETS BAY

Some say this is the best place for bathing on the island. It is small and separated by scattered rocks. Faces north east.

LONGY BAY

South east of the island. This large sandy beach is over-looked by Essex Castle. The east side is recommended for shrimping and prawning. Large smooth rocks are perfect for spreading yourself out and sunbathing on. To the west is Fort Raz island which boasts a privately owned oyster breeding colony. Nearby is Hanging Rock. There is a legend which relates that when rival islanders in Guernsey were intending to steal Alderney during the night they were going to attach a rope to this rock to tow it away. Faces south east.

TELEGRAPH BAY

A steep walk down a cliff road approaches this sandy beach. Do not bother to descend the steps unless the sea is at half tide or less. Watching the tide is tricky and once you are on the beach do watch out to avoid being cut off. The beach is surrounded by craggy rocks which are excellent for exploring. Sea caves behind provide endless enjoyment for exploration. Faces south.

SALINE BAY

This beach is north of the island and worth mentioning because bathing *is not recommended* here. Even under the best conditions there is a strong sea current and undertow.

CRABBY BAY

North east of Saline Bay. Sheltered by Fort Doyle prom-ontory to the west and Fort Grosnez near Braye Harbour breakwater to the east, it is fairly good for swimming. Some sand.

WALKING

There are numerous walks to be had round Alderney. One of the best times of year to visit is during spring when the headland glows with fresh wild flowers and yellow gorse which grows in abundance near the cliff edges. There are a number of landmarks to explore, and many of these provide excellent walking country between forts or German bunkers left since the last war.

There are a large number of forts on Alderney. They are all approachable but some have been converted into flats or holiday lets such as on Fort Clonque. Others have an interesting history such as Essex Castle. The building stands on a site which dates back to medieval times although the name was not introduced until the 19th century. It was once used as a military hospital and during the Second World War was altered by the German Occupying forces. Fort Clonque is now owned by the Landmark Trust and has been divided up into flats. The Monk's Chair nearby has a legend to explain its name. One night a monk fought the devil here, and won. The monk was so exhausted that when he sank into the sea the rocks around him miraculously transformed into a seat.

Many of the forts were built in the Victoria era, such as Fort Albert named after the Prince Consort. This building is 200 feet above sea level and was used as a barracks, until 1930, by the Alderney militia. Raz Island is another Victorian fort approachable by causeway at low water. The Germans added to it during the war. Fort Hournet Herbe is a Victorian fort which is partly ruined. Another fort you will probably visit is Fort Tourgis which is the second largest on the island. Nearby is a prehistoric cist which is the only surviving example on Alderney.

What to See

ST ANNES

St Anne's is the centre of Alderney and most of the population live there. Among early buildings are those built around Marais Street in the town. In the 18th century housewives did their laundry in a stream running alongside here and an original fountain and cattle trough still remain. Most of the houses in this square are 19th century and are very attractive. It is a friendly town, where people that you meet alway greet you with a 'hello'. Consequently it is difficult to remain a stranger in Alderney for very long. Most of the streets are cobbled and fairly narrow so drivers should be careful when parking as most of the streets are one way. Royal Connaught Square is one of the prettiet in the town. Nearby is Le Hurét which is the original site of the ancient parliament held in Alderney called the 'folk moot'. Royal proclamations and official news were declared from this site for centuries. The island States Buildings are in New Street and administration for the island is planned here. Parallel to the High Street are some of the oldest lanes in St Anne's. These 'venelles' were once tracks used by farmers who transported loads of 'Vraic' (or seaweed) to and from the shore to fertilise the land. One of the finest churches in the Channel Islands is St Anne's Parish Church. It is an imposing building which stands in fine grounds. When the bells ring out the whole village is alerted. The style of the church is early English and the stained glass windows depict local scenes and biblical subjects. Further out is the Butes. This is now a sports ground and a great bonfire is lit here every year at the end of Alderney week, which is during the first week in August. If you come and stay during this time you can join in the festivities and may even win an egg and spoon race. The name 'Butes' is derived from 'Butts' which originally meant a site for target practice.

TELEGRAPH TOWER
These are two giant rocks east of Telegraph Bay built during the Napoleonic Wars. They are each 100 feet high and are viewed best from the beach.

ALDERNEY MUSEUM Old School by Clock Tower, Lower High Street
The local museum is run by Reg Harris who used to be a senior scientific officer at the Natural History Museum in London. The museum consists of a vast open room with examples of geology and archaeology relating to Alderney. There are fine examples of wartime relics and one adjoining room contains a tableaux of a typical post war domestic setting in Alderney with examples of government issued furniture. Reg Harris is also building up a new natural history section. Open Monday-Saturday 10.00-12.30 am. The local Alderney Society has its HQ here.

ALDERNEY LIBRARY Island Hall, Royal Connaught Square
Visitors are welcome to use this library providing they pay a deposit for the books that they borrow. Open every weekday in the summer 10.00-12.30 am except Thursdays.

ALDERNEY LIGHTHOUSE Les Casquets

This is a famous working lighthouse which was built in 1912. Preceding this date the site has a history of vessels which crashed to smithereens on the dangerous rocks surrounding it. The rocks have been used for warning ships since the early 18th century. Before the modern lighthouse was erected the only method of keeping the lamps alight was with oil and taper. A family with six children manned it this way for 18 years. 'Les Casquets' is a poem written by Swinburne which describes the dangerous reefs. Today the new lighthouse is 120 feet high and has a visible radius of 17 miles. For visiting arrangements contact:
Alderney 25222

BURHOU ISLAND

This long green island is a favourite spot for birdwatchers and is only accessible by sea in a private boat. The hut on the island is rentable for £1 a night from the States Tourist Authority (see 'Where to Stay'). There are still traces of a cottage built in the 19th century which has never been inhabited since. Today it is uninhabited except for puffins, gulls and shags and the rabbits which burrow here. On a clear day the island is visible from Fort Clonque or the Butes. If you are lucky you may catch sight of some seals, oyster catchers or razor bills.

LES ETACS

Another name for this rock stack west of Alderney, is Garden Rocks. After the Second World War the islanders returned to find a new colony of gannets had inhabited them.

Sport

FISHING

Fishing from the shore can be good fun. If you need bait or tackle visit Beverley Rose Tackle shop in Victoria Street. This shop also organises *fishing trips* around the island that last about two hours. The boat will hold up to twelve people. Prices vary. Adults: £5.50 approximately. Children £3.00. Contact:

David Peacock during the day tel: Alderney 3279, and in the evening: tel: Alderney 3279

Diving for shellfish, lobsters or crabs is strictly prohibited.

SAILING

Sailing around Alderney can be dangerous and only experienced yachtsmen are encouraged to enter Braye Harbour. This is the safest anchorage on the island and there are about 50 moorings available for visitors. New arrivals should report to the Harbour Office on the quay. Some charge will be made for the use of mooring. Alderney Sail Club is at Braye Harbour and is open to members of other recognised sailing clubs. Facilities are available to the visiting yachtsman from: Mainbrayce Ltd., Inner Harbour, who offer service and repairs to visiting craft as well as fresh water at the berthing quay. Diesel fuel is also available. Rowing boats are for hire at £2 per day. Sailing dinghies cost £6.00 per half day. An alternative place for chandlery is at: The Sail Loft, Braye, St Annes tel: Alderney 2278. The Guernsey Brewery Company publish local tide tables and Alderney Sailing Club also issue 'Alderney Sailing Directions' which contain useful information for yachtsmen on local navigation routes etc. Contact:

Alderney Sailing Club, tel: Alderney 2748

WATER SPORTS ETC

There are no organised water sports on Alderney.

GOLF

There is a golf course on the island at Longy Common, but no other organised facilities for sport.

Your best bet is to ask at the nearest pub or hotel, what activities are currently 'going on' in Alderney at the time. There is no cinema on Alderney but films are shown occasionally during the summer in St Annes in the local hall.

Part IV
Sark

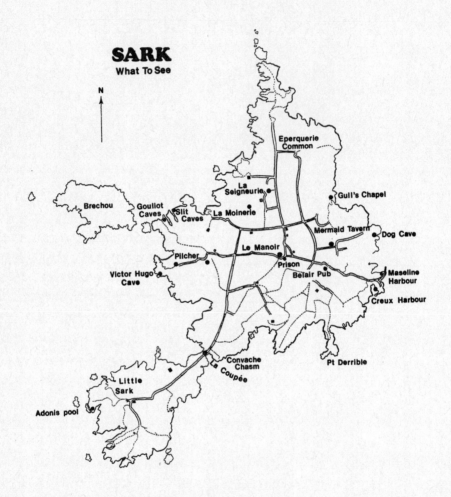

SARK
What To See

N

Eperquerie
Common

La
Seigneurie

Brechou

Gouliot
Caves

Slit
Caves

La Moinerie

Gull's Chapel

Mermaid Tavern

Dog Cave

Le Manoir

Pilcher

Prison

Victor Hugo
Cave

Belair Pub

Maseline
Harbour

Creux Harbour

Convache
Chasm

La Coupée

Pt Derrible

Little
Sark

Adonis pool

0   1 mile

The Island Today

Sark is one of the most picturesque of all the islands. There is something appealing about the tradition and life on it which attracts hundreds of visitors every year. Another feature is the close community life that exists here. Do not go to Sark expecting to find big hotels or luxurious tourist facilities. Often people come to Sark expecting to find all the amenities that they have paid to leave behind. Here there are no nightclubs and few pubs. Hotels and public houses there certainly are but the emphasis is on quality rather than quantity, and an appreciation that 'small is beautiful' will certainly be an added bonus.

The population on the island is a mixture of rich tax exiles and local residents. The core of the community revolves around the general running of the island, and because this is so close knit everybody has to be adaptable. The island tourist officer is Mrs Guilliard, once the principal lady at the local telephone exchange. Her husband is one of the two postmen employed on the island, which is a full time job he has performed daily for the last 10 years. There are no cars on the island and every day he wheels out his bicycle in all weathers to deliver the island post.

Unemployment is non existant here and everybody busies themselves either with farming, or with the tourist season which booms every summer. The island is adapting to modern life which some think is to its detriment. Instead of the old telephone exchange on the island, manned by individual telephone operators, a computerised machine has been installed. Now the system is fully automatic which some people feel is an intrusion on the island. At one time the island doctor used to rely on the telephone operator at the local exchange so he could be tracked down whilst on his daily rounds.

Most of the islanders express a natural aversion to urban living. Here a job is not just an occupation from 9-5 pm it is a way of life. The natural friendliness exuded from an islander is soon sapped by the impersonal face of a big city. Life is very different on Sark. Here everybody greets each other with a courteous 'good morning' whether you look like a stranger or not. It seems a natural thing to do on this tranquil little island. Here none of the roads are tarmacked. Instead of the continuous sound of traffic what you may hear during the quieter seasons is the occasional farm tractor, which is the only motorised vehicle permissible on the road. Most people go about their daily business quietly and unhurriedly on foot, or by bicycle.

Seeing a group of bicyclists appearing in two's or three's with shopping bags hanging precariously from their handlebars is a common occurrence. Elsewhere they may be left propped up against shopfronts or by the side of a house. At moments like this, particularly during the summer months when bicycles are hired out to visitors, the activity on the island seems to reach a feverish intensity. Additional transport is always laid on for visitors, but sadly fewer horsedrawn carriages are to be seen now. The last Dame of Sark strictly prohibited the use of any motor transport but today rules are more relaxed and 'carriages' which consist of three or four banks of seats with overhead cover are cunningly connected to tractors for the island tours.

During this time life on Sark seems closer to Shanghai. The arrival of tour operators on the island in recent years has made individual travel more difficult. Restaurants can be fully booked at mealtimes. For this reason it is advisable to ring prior to your visit. Such organisation seems off key on such a tiny island. Sark identifies so closely with natural harmony and excitement that a visit seems more like the exploration of a new planet or a tiny world. Talking to the inhabitants and seeing the way they live is certainly a fresh experience. Perhaps it is time that some of the city folk among us took a leaf out of their book, so as to fully appreciate the wonder of an environment 'famous', as one journalist has aptly stated, 'for its diminutives'.

SOME POINTS IN FAVOUR

The spectacular scenery on Sark and fascinating area for those interested in exploration. Sweet little cottages and old farm houses on Little Sark. Independence to be had travelling by bicycle and friendliness of the islanders.

SOME POINTS AGAINST

The small modern houses lining the avenue which gives this unique little island a high street which closely resembles an American film set. Excessive tourism in high summer. More tractors used to transport visitors than the genuine old pony and carriage.

WHAT TO BRING

If you plan to stay on Sark be sure to bring warm clothing. There are few shops here and most islanders travel to Guernsey to buy any luxuries. Don't forget to bring your camera.

A Short History

The name Sark has been traced back to Roman times. Then the island was probably known as Sarnia or Sarmia and with the other Channel Islands formed part of the Roman Empire. The island has been inhabited as long as as 3,000 BC. Neolithic remains have also been unearthed, and during the 19th century archaeologists excavating on the island discovered megalithic tombs. Unfortunately most of these are no longer in existence. During the days of their discovery many were removed from their original sites or even broken up and used as building materials.

During Roman times Sark was a trading station. Coins have been discovered here, but little remains to indicate signs of any settlement on the island. The arrival of Christianity was of special significance to Sark. Whether any one person was responsible is still not clear. Saint Maglorius emerges as the chief saint connected with the island, and is said to have founded a monastery, 'La Moinerie' or the Monastery near to La Seigneurie on the north west of the island. A community was established there which flourished for some time, surviving by working on the land and educating the children of local nobility in the diocese.

The arrival of the Vikings from Scandinavia in the

north was the cause of considerable change in all the islands. Sark was ruthlessly invaded, and today there are no remains to be seen of the monastery that was originally established. What was to emerge was a new settlement when the Norse invaders eventually stayed peaceably in the lands they had conquered. Their leader was called Rollo and when he signed the Treaty of St Clair sur Epte he was given Normandy in return for his services and the promise that he would defend his lands and recognise Charles the Simple as his sovereign. In 933 his son Duke William was given lands that included the present Channel Islands.

The successive Dukes were responsible for the administration on the islands and organised their property into fiefs. Each fief had a lord or a Seigneur and the local inhabitants were answerable to him and paid their taxes in return for the use of his lands. Sark was granted firstly to the abbey of Mont St Michel in 1042 and later to the Bishop of Coutances in 1057. The invasion of England in 1066 by Duke William II, and his accession to the English throne, started an association with the Channel Islands which was to remain unbroken, except in a few instances until the present day. During the reign of his various successors Sark was first granted to Geoffrey Monbrai, Bishop of Coutances. After he fell from favour the island was later pased to successive rival dukes (depending on who had kept control of their Norman lands). During the 12th century immigrants were encouraged to settle on the island which introduced a period of expansion and prosperity. The community settled around the ancient site of St Maglorius' monastery and their religious welfare was looked after by a Parish priest in the area of La Seigneurie, still under the instruction of the Bishop of Coutances. It was in the mid 12th century that the same site was donated to the Abbey of Mounteborg by a Norman baron called William de Dernon. As was the fashion for the wealthy of this period a large sum of money was set aside for an Abbey to maintain a hermit to say prayers for the good of the Baron's soul and his immediate family. This tradition was maintained for generations.

When the King succeeded to the English throne in 1199 the lands in Normandy were lost to the French King Phillipe Auguste, but the Channel Islands remained loyal to him, even though Sark was captured twice by the French. However 34 hostages were taken by King John to ensure the alliegance of the island and secure his own political ambitions. From this moment onward the island was constantly prone to invasion, and early fortifications were built around this time to defend the islands against attacks from Normandy. Throughout the 13th century Sark remained relatively trouble free. The Lord of the Isles was delegated to administer justice and the collection of revenue for the Crown. Six jurats chosen from the local community assisted in the administration of justice as well as six jurors who were enrolled, with the help of itinerant judges sent by the Crown. There were about 300 people living on Sark at this time and each household donated two hens every year in tax, as well as corn, which was paid in tithes to the appropriate monastic houses. Most of the islanders survived by farming, fishing and trading rabbit skins.

The 14th century marked the beginning of a decline on the island. The Hundred Years War, which had started in 1338 in the reign of King Edward III, opened a period of bitter conflict between England and France. The Channel Islands were still loyal to the English Crown, but were literally 'sandwiched' between the two countries, and were regarded by both as strategic property in time of war. Sark was captured by Nicholas Béhuchet, Admiral of France, who occupied it for two years. The island was freed when King Edward III won the battle of Stuys in 1340, and restored it to its former position under English control. The warden Thomas de Ferrers manned the island, with a small number of men for its defence, but these measures were not sufficient. The island was captured again in 1343 and occupied for four years. A further tragedy hit the island when the Black Death that had swept Europe reached the island in 1348. Peace returned to the islands in 1360 when the Treaty of Calais restored the islands to the English Crown. However none of these bids for peace lasted for very long. Sark was recaptured by the French between 1372 and 1375 and the damage done was so severe that the local community was completely wiped out. No attempt was made to resettle the island, and the land was abandoned except for grazing and rabbit hunting. It also provided a refuge for privateers.

The island had already suffered so many losses that the agreement between England and France to treat the Channel Islands as neutral territory in 1483 came too late since it was already ravaged. By the beginning of the 16th century widespread changes were sweeping through Europe. The schism with the Roman Catholic Church and the Reformation during the reign of Henry VIII brought changes which were even to be seen on the islands. Also the rise of protestantism in France resulted in many French Hugenots turning to the Channel Islands as an alternative place of refuge. Sark was considered by the French to be strategic because by this time it was uninhabited and relatively easy to capture. Also the possession of the Channel Islands was still contested, as the French insisted that they were part of Normandy which had been restored to them long ago. In 1548 an attempt was made to repopulate the island. It was invaded with 200 men and the French remained in control until 1553. An attempt was then made by a Flemish General Adrian Cole to capture Sark and repopulate the island in the name of Emperor Charles V. However it was a futile attempt. The island was too insignificant to impress the Emperor who already had so much in his possession. England was undergoing widespread religious changes under the new reign of Queen Mary. Protestant Huguenots were escaping from the Channel Islands elsewhere and the English government was hardly in a position to be alarmed at the fate of this tiny island. Faced with such apathy and unable to negotiate with England for the repossession of the island in exchange for payment Cole withdrew his troops.

The next attempt to occupy Sark was by the French in 1560. They abandoned when war broke out between France and England in 1562. The accession of Queen Elizabeth I in England assured safety for Huguenot protestants again in the islands and also the re-establishment of the Presbyterian religion. Interest was revived in Sark again by Helier de Carteret, Seigneur of St Ouen in 1563. He envisaged a plan of re-populating Sark, not only to keep it as an English possession, but also to ensure the safety of any of the other islands still open to attack once the island had become enemy territory. By 1565 peace was declared between England and France. The first plans for settlement were introduced and letters patent from the Queen strengthened his position. Helier de Carteret was responsible for re-settling the island with at least 40 men who were English and obedient to the Crown. This ingenious plan was the basis of island land division still to be seen today.

Le Manoir was built as Helier de Carteret's property and 39 other plots of land were leased out with attractive low rents to the colonists. By these methods he had acquired enough householders to form a community, who were armed to defend the island. One of the original divisions which he created still survives from this period: Beauregard on the south west of the island, so called because of the fine view to be had over to Guernsey. The roads of the island also date from this time. Many of the settlers came from Jersey. Once the settlement was established in 1570 Helier was presented with Sark, including Brechou. His son Philippe inherited authority over the island in 1578. The administration of the island was adopted along the lines of Jersey law. This was all the more appropriate since most of the new inhabitants were from Jersey and used to its methods. A bailiff and 12 jurats were appointed and a court of justice set up after much opposition from the Guernsey Court. After much wrangling the people responsible for implementing this new system were imprisoned for setting up an illegal court. It was not until 1583 that details were finalised.

Even though Sark had always been subordinate to Guernsey only 5 jurats were appointed from the local community to manage civil affairs after these new land reforms. Other administrative problems arose over the question of land tenure to safeguard the existing tenements and prevent subdivision of properties. In this way differences also arose concerning suffrage and the building of property on the island by succeeding generations. It was important to preserve these properties and to draw up provisions for defending the island. The Seigneur eventually obtained letters patent from King James I in 1611 which altered the original agreements drawn up under Elizabeth I. The result of these new documents was that each unit of land was to pass to a direct heir, or be sold intact, and the building of new property was limited. One feature of the new law was 'Retrait' which gave a relative the right to buy back property, purchased within 40 days of sale, from the original buyer. The provision still exists today and in varying forms on the other islands. The basis of land tenure was secured and this system, in a variant form, is still used today. The inhabitants continued to thrive, living off the fruits of farming, cidermaking, and fishing. Also vraic gathering and knitting started as an island industry from this time.

During the Civil War, Sark followed the puritan cause with Guernsey, whilst Jersey was firmly Royalist. Fighting broke out between the islands and an attack was made on Sark in 1644. After the restoration in 1650 the internal politics of the island continued to be fought, between successive generations of ruling families until the accession of William of Orange in 1689. The Declaration of War on France, was worsened because the Papal Bull of Neutrality was cancelled by the Order of Council in 1689 which ensured that the islands would not provide safe refuge to James or his French supporters. The outbreak of war encouraged new privateering ventures on a massive scale.

During the 18th century the islanders had amassed so much wealth from trading and privateering that there was enough surplus money to be spent on rebuilding parts of the town. The majority of houses in St Anne are Georgian in style and date from this period. The Le Pelley family held the fief of Sark throughout the 18th century and organised the general running of the island. By 1796 Methodism had reached the islands and a chapel was built. Later during the Napolonic wars a barracks provided a much needed addition to island defence. At the beginning of the 19th century a new school house was built and in 1832 a prison stood waiting to house any of the new influx of quarry workers who committed an offence.

In 1834 a mining company was set up by a certain John Hunt, a surveyor, and the Seigneur Le Pelley. The search for silver ore brought employment to the island. The Guernsey and Sark Mining Company was one of two companies instigated by Hunt; the other, Herm Mining Company, was started in 1837 to mine for copper. Although operations ticked over for a while, the venture was not particularly successful and by 1847 the Guernsey and Sark Mining Company had ceased to function. The Seigneur lost considerable amounts of money and this financial misadventure cost him his fief. His relatives were forced to sell the property which exchanged hands in 1852 and was sold to a west country family called Collings. The Reverend William Thomas Collings succeeded his mother at Seigneur in 1853.

A new industry, tourism, was beginning to emerge by the mid 19th century. The arrival of the Romantic era, evidenced by Swinburne's poems and the writing of Victor Hugo promoted its interest, for both were frequent visitors to the island. As communications improved, so did the number of visitors on the regular steam vessels departing from the busy port of Southampton. In 1857 Sark's communications improved, when the first post office was established. Once this isolated island was open to English speaking visitors, including the influx of miners from Cornwall, the French patois ceased to be the island language. The number of inhabitants dropped steadily as industry and agriculture on the island declined. Before and after the First World War interest in Sark as a tax haven began to intensify. Soon the original houses and tenements were passing to non-residents. The attraction of low income tax, and the avoidance of death duty, increased in later years and the population on Sark was changed dramatically by the new influx of residents.

William Collings died in 1927 and was succeeded by his daughter Sybil. She married a Mr Beaumont, and then an American, Roger Hathaway, who was to become naturalized as a British subject. Famous for her forthright character, the Dame promoted the island and increased its revenue through tourism. She also earned a considerable reputation for the handling of island affairs during the war, whilst the Germans were occupying the island. 1965 marked the 400th anniversary of the charter granted to Helier de Carteret by Elizabeth I, and the system that was introduced then has changed little today. Various changes have been discussed to facilitate modern living, such as changes in the law regarding land tenure, simply to protect the island against the ravages of the 20th century. Dame Sybil Hathaway was succeeded by her grandson, Michael Beaumont, in 1974. As the present Signeur he has the task of guiding the island towards the 21st century.

How to get to the Island

By Sea

Sark is only accessible by boat, although in an emergency small aircraft or a helicopter are allowed to land. The Isle of Sark Shipping Co., send out up to 7 boats daily from St Peter Port. The Isle of Sark is a cargo boat which sets out daily at 7.00 am from Guernsey on the 'milk run'. The trip takes about one hour in an old fashioned white painted vessel, with gleaming brass and excessive petrol fumes. Not advisable for anybody prone to sea sickness, but a great way of meeting people on their way to work. Price for a return ticket is £4.50 leaving daily at 10.00am excepting Sundays. For more details contact:

Isle of Sark Shipping Company, White Rock, St Peter Port, Guernsey. tel: Guernsey 24059; or
Isle of Sark Shipping Company, The Knoll, Rue Lucas, Sark. tel: Sark 10
Commodore run a hydrofoil service between all the islands. There is usually one every day between all the islands and sometimes more. Check for details from:
Jersey Commodore Shipping Services Ltd., 28 Conway Street, Albert Quay, St Helier. tel: Jersey 71263 or
Guernsey Commodore Shipping Services Ltd, North Pier Steps, St Peter Port, Guernsey, tel; Guernsey 26121.

Travel within the Island

by car 220   by bicycle 220   island tours 221

By Car

Cars are not allowed on Sark. There are no buses, and no
public transport. The only motor vehicles on the island are
tractors. These are mainly used for farming. However
when landing as Maseline or Creux Harbour visitors will
find these vehicles transformed into 'motor carriages'. This
is a solution to the practical problem of transporting
visitors, and their luggage, up to the steep hill in relative
comfort – for a small charge.

Bicycle

Once on the island the most popular way of getting to
places is by bike. These are on hire from Jackson's Toy

Store or the Post Office in the Avenue for just £1 per day. Be prepared to pay a deposit and always *return the bicycle* at the end of the day. These are available for hire all the year round.

Island Tours

Apart from the motorised carriages mentioned above, the old form of horse and cart is a popular method of touring the island. Traditionally, these were the only form of transport for hundreds of years. Today there are still a few which can be hired on arrival at Maseline Harbour for tours of the island which last about one hour.

Where to Stay

hotels and guest houses p223 caravans and camping p224
Eating and Entertainment p224

Sark operates on a seasonal basis which means that few hotels are open in the winter. The Tourist Information Officer has the current list of up to date bed and breakfast or self catering accommodation. Contact:
Mrs Guilliard, tel: Sark 135 for information.
The system in Sark is not to grade accommodation. It is best to work out your requirements exactly before making a choice. The function of the Tourist Officer is to provide impartial information, not to offer recommendations. If you need to make a choice approach the problem by saying, 'If you were in my position which one would you choose? In all cases early bookings are essential.

The following hotels and guest houses are all well established on the island and offer a good range of what you may expect to find. Prices given for accommodation are only approximate and for a single person staying at half board unless stated otherwise. Restaurant prices are also approximate and for one person including wine unless stated otherwise.

Hotels and Guest Houses

AVAL DU CREAUX HOTEL Harbour Hill, tel Sark 2036
This hotel is a 16th century granite building which overlooks the sea. All facilities are provided such as hot and cold water etc. It is also mentioned in the Good Food Guide. Prices start at £16 for dinner, bed and breakfast. The restaurant is open to non-residents and a set 3 course lunch costs £3.80 not including wine. A 4 course dinner can cost £6.00 not including wine.

BEAUVOIR GUEST HOUSE Rue de la Moinerie, tel: Sark 2082
This hotel is near to the Seigneurie and is unlicensed. As well as having a pleasant stay very good cream teas can be had in the garden during the summer, except on Sundays. The price for bed and brakfast here is very reasonable at £10. Packed lunches are also available.

DIXCART HOTEL Dixcart Lane, tel: Sark 2001
This old granite house is the longest established hotel on the island. There is hot and cold water and some rooms have private bathrooms attached. There is a dining room, a bar and even a private library, spanning two rooms. Mentioned in the Good Food Guide for it's excellent cuisine. Bed and breakfast prices start at £16.00 rising to £19.50 during the high season. The price of a 3 course lunch costs £4.50 not including wine. Dinner in the restaurant starts at £5.50 for 3 courses or à la carte.

STOCKS HOTEL Dixcart Lane, tel: Sark 2001

This hotel has a good reputation. It has a swimming pool and you can also book for bed and breakfast, which costs £17.50-£20.50 during the high season. There is a lunchtime buffet served from 10am-6pm or you can choose a 4 course meal, main dish steak and chips can cost £2.50. At dinner there is a wide choice and one example of the price of a good steak or delicious lobster is £6.00 not including wine.

Caravans and Camping

Caravans are not permitted on Sark and there are no authorised camping sites.

Eating and Entertainment

Visitors arriving at Maseline Harbour have a choice of two places to stop and eat at on their way through the island. The Mermaid Tavern and Belair Pub are both packed in summer and the first place you will get a decent drink and a snack from when you arrive. The other main eating places are for when you feel like splashing out, at the hotels previously listed.

Leisure Activities

the beaches p225   walking p227   sports p229

The Beaches

Swimming in Sark is exciting because the benefits are two fold. If you get tired of it then there are rocky faces for adventurous scramblers to climb, or rocky pools for idle exploration of Sark sea water life.

The beaches on Sark are never really crowded. Most are easily scrambled to and the only thing to watch out for are the tides. Tide tables are available from the Guernsey Press Company Limited and these are especially useful because they contain information about the spring tides.

CREAUX HARBOUR
'Creux' mean hole or cave and this sandy harbour is safe for swimming. East of the island.

DERRIBLE BAY
This beach is popular perhaps because it has easy access. It is also very safe for swimming and has a gently shelving

beach which exposes sand at low tide and is very attractive to family bathers. Faces south.

L'EPERQUERIE LANDING
Is a man made pool north of the island, suitable for children. If you are a strong swimmer it is a fine place to strike out from beyond the landing.

LES FONTAINES BAY
Near to the Fern Cave and Fairy Grotto this beach is best to swim in at high tide when the water level is high enough to avoid dangerous rocks. Faces north west.

GRANDE GRÈVE
This is one of the islands largest beaches. It is immensely popular and beautiful sands face the Atlantic. It is accessible via a steep path leading down from Le Coupee. It is also famous for the 'Sark Stones' rarely found today : raw amethysts, emeralds and agates have all been found here in their uncut state. Faces north west.

LE GRÈVE DE LA VILLE
North of the island this beach is rocky when the tide is lower than half level. It is accessible via an easy winding descent on foot. Towards the south coast is a cave called 'Fat man's misery. If you cannot crawl straight through from one end to the other then you know it is time to diet. Other mysterious natural caves are the Gulls Chapel and Dog Caves. Faces north east.

HAVRE GOSSELIN
Northeast of Sark and facing Brechou island. This is near to the Pilcher monument which was erected in memory of a man who drowned off the point. There is a small landing

jetty for bathing and fishing. Southward is a small group of prominent rocks called 'The Slobberers'. If you listen to the noise that the water makes around then you will soon find out the reason for their name.

PORT DU MOULIN

This is a north west facing shingly beach which is safe for bathing at low tide. 'Les Autelets' (little altars) are three granite columns which provide sheltered bathing at low tide.

ROUGE TERRIER BAY

South east of little Sark. Bathing here is at half to high tide. Especially good for picnics as there are large smooth rocks to spread yourselves out and sunbathe on.

SAIGNIE BAY

The name means Bay of Blood. It is north west of the island and very good for bathing. Great for exploring the surrounding cliffs.

VENUS POOL

This is a natural circular rocky pool on Little Sark which is only 18 feet deep. At high tide the water covers the smooth stones. These have been naturaly 'sculpted' by the movement of water around them. Deep diving is possible from the rocks at the east and south sides. Faces south east.

Walking

Walking on Sark is relaxing. It is $1\frac{1}{2}$ miles wide by 3 miles long and separated by La Coupée, a narrow natural viaduct with treacherous rocks below. La Coupée divides the main island from little Sark, on a clear day the view is quite breathtaking. The rocky cliffs fall for hundreds of feet below into clear blue water with strong powerful waves. On a clear day you can see France on one side, and Guernsey on the other. Sark is famous for its beauty and tranquility but the best time to visit is in spring. There are fewer visitors then, the air is fresh and clear, spectacular wild flowers, such as primroses, wild bluebells and hyacinths abound. In the late summer, roads get hot and dusty and the island can also be very crowded.

There are many footpaths on Sark, but no rights of way. Any diversion onto private property must be with care and consideration since most routes to the beaches are through private land. Eperquerie Common, near to the landing, is a good place for picnics. (L'Epoerquerie was the original name for sites used in medaevil times for drying/curing catches of conger). It is good for exploring caves around here, but always watch out for the tides. The Fairy Grotto, is named after a painting by William Topliss, RA who lived for a time in Jersey and on Sark and had several of his paintings exhibited between 1875-1902 at the Royal Academy. When the sun is overhead the rocks can look like a woman arched with trailing draperies. There is also 'Fern Cave' named by the same artist. Southwards, is red cave or drinking horse cave. 'Creux' or shafts cut in the rocks run vertically down from the rock face, surrounding a central rock which resembles a drinking horse. There are numerous caves along the northern face of the island and all their names are individual. Dog Cave for instance is so called because of the barking noise that can be heard, which is due to the combination of tidal level and airy cross currents.

Sport

There are no organised sports on Sark. Any enquiries should be directed to the Tourist Information Office, tel: Sark 135.

Sark is ideal for scramblers. Some of you may never have heard of this peculiar activity and may only associate the word with eggs. However, this precarious pastime is peculiar to this tiny island with a coast region of 42 miles. Here the energetic can easily scramble along the caves and rocky inlets to their heart's content. There is an art of scaling the rocks in rapid style and enjoyment improves with practice and ingenuity. Derrible Head is ideal, but only at low tide. Beware of Suicides Leap, between the headland and Petit Derrible Bay, named after the steep cliffs which reached dizzy heights and are tempting to those with short sharp shocks in mind.

Venus Pool on the south east coast of little Sark is famous and great for swimming. The best time is about two hours either side of low water, before 11 in the morning. Another beauty spot, named after the gods is, Adonis Pool which is circular and natural and about 18 feet deep near Fontaine Bay on the north coast of the island. La Coupée is spectacular and has wonderful views of Jersey and Guernsey to the west and Brechou Island. Another feature here is Convache Chasm with its extraordinary coloured stone, seen best on a sunlit day. A magnificent view can be seen from the Pilcher monument which was erected on Longue Point headland facing Brechou. Victor Hugo Cave cannot be visited without a guide since the area is dangerous and great caution is advised if a visit is planned. The cave is about 35 metres in length and a huge entrance open out into a cavern. Further to the north, the Gouilot caves can be found. They are fascinating to visit, if only because their remote situation makes them accessible only in low or spring tides. The slit caves are followed by the Jewel Cave which is clustered with glistening sea anemones. These caves were once used to store the contraband of privateers.

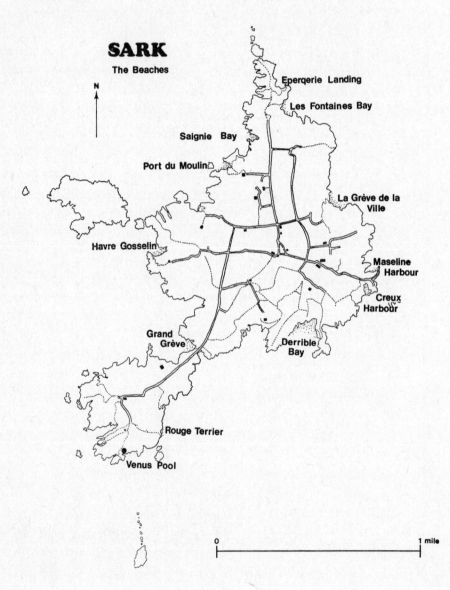

SARK
The Beaches

N

Eperqerie Landing

Les Fontaines Bay

Saignie Bay

Port du Moulin

La Grève de la Ville

Havre Gosselin

Maseline Harbour

Creux Harbour

Grand Grève

Derrible Bay

Rouge Terrier

Venus Pool

0   1 mile

Part V
Herm

HERM

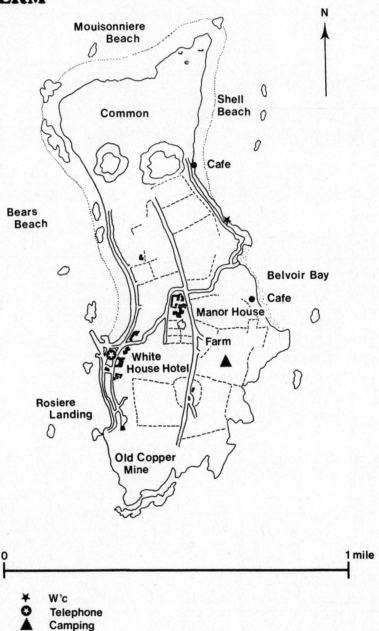

N

Mouisonniere
Beach

Shell
Beach

Common

Cafe

Bears
Beach

Belvoir Bay

Cafe

Manor House

Farm

White
House Hotel

Rosiere
Landing

Old Copper
Mine

| 0 | | 1 mile |

✱   W'c
✪   Telephone
▲   Camping

The Island Today

The next best thing to owning a private island must be staying on one, especially if it happens to be tranquil with idyllic beaches and only twenty miles from the French coast of Brittany. Herm is one of the smallest Channel Islands with a sizeable reputation. It has been described as an 'earthly paradise'. Although this is a tiny island measuring only one and a half miles long by half a mile wide it has a variety of features to attract the visitor. The wide expanse of 'shell beach' which flanks the east coast has made Herm famous. To some it evokes heady visions of an island in the South Seas, especially, as a journalist once cracked, for people who have never seen one.

The present owner, Major Peter Wood, took over the position of tenant in 1949. When you visit Herm all that can be seen is the result of 30 years hard and careful work. Now the island flourishes both as an agricultural and a business concern, which is quite a contrast from the way he inherited it. Major Wood runs the island with his family, employing permanent and temporary staff to run the hotel and manage the farm. There is a full time teacher employed to supervise the local school, which accepts pupils at primary school age. There are seldom more than eight in a class and the older children have to leave the island to be educated in Guernsey. In winter the population on Herm is about 40, swelling to as many as 300 in the summer season when visitors come to the island in large numbers.

There are about one hundred Guernsey cows grazing on 15 acres of cultivated land; they produce milk that is exported to Guernsey daily. The whole island is run as a company and as a financial concern. However, at the same time people who visit the island stay as guests, not as 'tourists' or 'trippers'. There is a unique family atmosphere on Herm. There are no councils, waterboards or dustmen to clear the garbage. Everything is privately catered for. The result is that standards are exceptionally high whilst every effort is made to please.

When you arrive in Herm you will land on the jetty. A path has been built from here to the central main buildings, which consist of the White House Hotel, two shops, and places to eat and drink. Daily visitors can have a drink in a pub converted from stables; it has a homely atmosphere and provides light meals. For people wishing to stay on the island there is a choice between the hotel, the self catering cottages available, or using your own camping facilities.

For anybody contemplating a holiday or who appreciates 'getting away from it all' this tiny locality may be just the place for you.

SOME POINTS IN FAVOUR
Herm Island is one of the few in the world which allows you to enjoy the experience of what it must be like to live on a private island of your own. There are exceptionally high standards and pleasant staff. The hotel is very comfortable and in ideal surroundings.

SOME POINTS AGAINST
None

WHAT TO BRING
Everything. You can easily travel across to Guernsey if you need to buy anything that has been left at home.

A Short History

Visitors to the island date as far back as Neolithic times, between 4,000 and 2,400 BC. Various sites have been discovered to indicate that early communities survived on Herm. Examples of finds are: standing stones and pottery, axes, megalithic structures built to contain ritualistic offerings or small collections of hunting implements, and sea shells piled in large numbers. The vast expanse of common to the north of the island has a mysterious past. Sixteen burial sites have been excavated on this tract of land and several stone burial chambers. When these tombs were first excavated in the middle of the last century by Lukis, a renowned archaeologist of the period, standards were not meticulous. The significance of many findings was not fully realised and as a result inadequate records of their discovery were made. Modern archaeologists are lacking in sufficient evidence of what the original discoveries amounted to in this sandy area.

A theory has been expounded that Herm might once have been a burial ground for the chieftains in the neighbouring isle of Brittany, who were conveyed here and ceremoniously buried with their sacrificial victims. Roman remains have also been discovered, but there is little evidence to support a theory that there were any settled communities. Herm was more likely to have served as a trading station for traffic passing between Gaul, England or Ireland. The original name of Herm was probably derived from this source. 'Herma' translated from Latin means 'deserted territory'. Other romantic sources contend that the island owes its name to a twelfth century hermit who inhabited the island.

In the 15th century Herm was connected with the neighbouring island of Jethou, on which St Magloire is reputed to have built a chapel, which was later destroyed by a storm. Remains of this little chapel survived well into the last century. There is an island church near the manor, which dates back to 1050 AD and many island people profess to have seen the ghost of a Franciscan monk. Robert, Duke of Normandy gave the island to an Augustinian order in Cherbourg, who founded a monastery. The walls of the original building still survive and are now incorporated as part of the present manor. This religious community of Herm flourished. It was referred to as 'the parochial church of St Tugal of Herm' in records that date back as far as 1480.

Herm has a maturity lacking in most other islands similar in size. Few others have such a rich history. The Norman occupation formed most of the legislation on the island and a court of officials was raised over the several hundred inhabitants. A major influence on the island was the loss of Normandy by King John in 1204. The islanders remained loyal to him and in so doing became intrinsically involved in the defence of England. Herm was a prime target from the coast of Normandy. As interest in the islands declined and the event of war became less frequent so the population in Herm dwindled. By 1569 Herm was annexed to the see of Winchester. By the beginning of the 17th century the community that had once flourished on the island was extinct.

Interest in Herm revived at the beginning of the 19th century. The Industrial Revolution encouraged the introduction of mining on the island when John Hunt started up a mining company at the beginning of the 19th century. Although this venture was short lived the island yielded a rich supply of granite instead, which provided an income for many workers who had initially been attracted by the mining industry. A prison survives from this time: it measures four metres in diameter and is said to be the smallest in the world. Obviously some form of jurisdiction was needed because by 1850, 400 people are recorded as living on the island. Herm granite became a material that was not only useful but very much sought after. The steps of Carlton House Terrace are an example of it in London.

In 1867 the island was leased to Colonel Fielden. This wealthy businessman spent considerable sums on buildings and converted the island into a private estate. Subsequent tenants have found this an appealing prospect, not least Prince Blucher Von Waklstatt, who became tenant from 1890. This eccentric millionaire took over the lease of the island and made roads, cultivated the gardens and even introduced wallabies to Herm, which numbered 40 at one time. Other famous tenants of Herm were Sir Compton Mackenzie, the novelist, and Lord Perry of the Ford Motor Company took over until the outbreak of the Second World War.

The Germans occupied the Channel Islands in June 1940 and Herm was used as pasture to fatten cattle and sheep. Only six people remained to look after the island, including the caretaker and his wife. The German infantry used Herm Common as practise ground for tank and landing exercises and also made a film entitled 'Invasion of the Isle of Wight' which they later showed in Germany for propaganda purposes. At the end of the war the island was bought from the Crown by the States of Guernsey. It was first let to the late Mr Jeffries on two conditions. Firstly the public should be allowed to land during daylight and secondly all the natural attractions should be preserved. With these two factors in mind and with most of the buildings in dismal need of repair the present owner Major Peter Wood took over the position of tenant on the island in 1949.

How to get to the Island

By Sea

This is the only practical way to get to Herm. There is a regular service in summer by hydrofoil which leaves Guernsey from the Clock Tower in St Peter Port. Visitors from Guernsey should enquire for sailing times from TRIDENT who have a kiosk at Weighbridge Clock Tower. tel: Guernsey 21379/45129. Other places to contact:

HERM SEAWAY (Opposite town church in St Peter Port). tel: Guernsey 24161

The cost of a return trip costs £3.00 and takes you to the landing steps at Herm Harbour or to La Rosiere Steps a quarter mile south at low tide.

Where to Stay

For visitors wishing to stay on Herm, either in self catering cottages, camping or in the hotel, it is advisable to contact either:

THE WHITE HOUSE Herm Island, via Guernsey C. Islands , tel: 0481-22159, or,

GUERNSEY & HERM LEISURE TRAVEL LIMITED Weighbridge Travel Centre, Lower Pollet, St Peter Port, Guersney, C. Islands, tel: 0481-21897.

Ask for details of their inclusive holidays, this will give you a comprehensive selection of what the island has to offer in accommodation and the total price including air/train and sea travel arrangements. Prices vary according to the time of year. Low season is from 14th September through to 21st May, high season is from 22nd May to 13th September. Hotel prices include 3 meals a day, breakfast, lunch and dinner, full board accommodation plus insurance, and approximate prices range from £21.50-£22.80 per person daily.

Hotel

The only hotel on the island is the **White House**; the hotel, which is large and comfortable was built in the last century and recently renovated. Each bedroom has a superb view, with a private bathroom, radio intercom and baby alarm. You can either have a room in the main hotel, or stay in rooms adjacent to the main building. Prices for these cottages range from £18.50-£24.50. The hotel is comfortably furnished and has a country atmosphere which is pleasant and a relief from chrome and aluminium fittings found in many hotels. There are some cheaper rooms without adjoining bathrooms. Picnic lunches are available on request. No dogs are allowed on the island.

Trident Kiosk, St Peter Port, Guernsey, tel: 21379 has a blackboard inside which shows the time of the next boat. Last trips daily at 5 pm. Special arrangements can be made for passengers arriving by Sealink in Guernsey, providing you notify the hotel.

Self Catering

Self catering accommodation on the island is popular and very limited, so it is advisable to book well in advance. Again prices are inclusive of travel, either by air from Southampton or sea from Weymouth. There are two cottages available, one for two and one for numbers up to eight. Contact the White House for details.

Camping

Camping holidays are adjusted according to whether or not you wish to hire equipment or bring your own. Prices include hire and use of site, if applicable, hire of tent, equipment and site fees.

Leisure Activities

The Beaches

SHELL BEACH

This is the main beach on Herm, it is on the north west side, and the most famous. One advantage of bathing there is for the magnificent view, another is the promise of exploration it provides. At one time many people visiting the islands left clutching exotic shells which reputedly arrived washed up on the shore swept by the currents of the Gulf stream. Today the same chances of acquiring such a free gift are slim. Most of the genuine articles have already been picked up, or dashed to tiny fragments by rolling waves long before any visitor can lay claim to them.

BELVOIR BAY

This is the most sheltered beach at the north end of the island. It is accessible via a high cliff walk and a steep downward path which leads to the rocks below. As it is sheltered from strong winds it is a popular place for bathing. There is a WC close by and the only refreshment kiosk on the island is further along the beach.

North of the island **MONISONNIERE BEACH** leads westwards to **THE BEARS BEACH** and as you walk around further in an anti-clockwise direction **FISHERMAN'S BEACH** lies first opposite the White House Hotel and Herm Harbour.

Commercial entertainment is not encouraged on Herm. Instead visitors can make use of the island's natural beauty spots. Most leisure activities are definitely of a homely nature. Barbecues and bonfires are sometimes organised on a fine night and these are extremely popular. People who stay on the island soon get to know one another and lively picnics are the order of the day. Staying on Herm is an experience you are not likely to forget. On this island you can shrug off the old habits of automatic entertainment, achieved on the mainland by a flick of a switch. Instead you can take a stroll and enjoy this tiny place simply for the peace and quiet that it provides, which you are not likely to find so easily anywhere else.

Eating and Entertainment

Herm is such a tiny island that there is not an enormous variety of places in which to eat. However, there is enough choice provided at the hotel and the surrounding area to satisfy a variety of tastes and price ranges. For daily visitors, arriving on the boat from Guernsey, a short walk to the centre of the island, past the continental style shops, will lead them to a charming little pub. This has been converted from an old stable block and has a pleasant rustic atmosphere, ideal for a light snack and a cool pint of beer. Outside chairs and tables are set out during the summer season. Next door is a restaurant which provides slightly more expensive meals such as quick hamburgers or a salad.

Towards the centre of the island the White House Hotel provides meals for residents and non-residents alike. There is a three course meal or a choice of self service alongside the main restaurant. The service is excellent and the surroundings are comfortable and homely. The restaurant also provides dinner in the evening.

What to See

You can easily walk around Herm island in an afternoon as it is only $\frac{1}{2}$ mile long and $\frac{1}{2}$ mile wide at its maximum point. But do not under estimate this island just because of its small size. There are many different scenes to walk through ranging from the lush pasture on the centre of the island to the fresh white shell beach on the headland. The Germans used this area to shoot propaganda films during the war, and it still inspires professional and amateur photographers today. Inland across grassy sand dunes is a flat sandy area that was used as a golf course before the First World War by the last island tenant. Once this area was a burial ground for the ancient kings of Brittany. They were rowed across the water and ceremoniously buried here because it was believed that their dead spirits could not retrace the route back across the straits, and thus were unable to haunt their dubious successors. This vicinity is still well known for strange phenomena and people have reported peculiar sightings here. Closer to the jetty near the hotel is the smallest prison in the world. Drinkers beware! You may be detained here for a night if you misbehave.

Some parts of the central buildings date back to medieval times. One wall of the manor once formed part of the old monastery and the island even claims to have a monastic ghost which has presented itself to a number of visitors in the past. There is also a small chapel in which regular services are held throughout the summer. Any proficient organist visiting Herm is encouraged to play on the organ during the weekend at the Sunday Service.

There is a farm on the island which produces enough milk to be transported daily to Guernsey. Walking through the fields can take you past the farmland and on so tiny an island you may be surprised to find yourself walking in such a rural setting. There is a camping site nearby.

Part VI
Miscellanea

Uninhabited Islands

The Ecrehous

Pronounced 'Ek-cree-hose' these three main rocky islets lie north west of Jersey half way between the island and the coast of France. They can best be seen from Rozel or further east near St Catherines' breakwater. Although the islands are uninhabited today there are stone huts still to be seen which were erected by wealthy residents on the island during the last century. These are sometimes used in the summer months by Jersey residents. Maître Isle, Marmotière and Blanc Ile were inhabited during prehistoric times but today all that remains to be seen are a few houses and cottages built during the 19th century. The ruins of a priory still remain on Marmotière and even the old Customs House which once flourished is partially standing. The last resident of the Ecrehous was a Jerseyman called Philip Pinal. He lived on the islands for many years during the last century and was known as 'King of the Ecrehous'.

The Minquiers

These reefs are pronounced 'Minkies' and form part of the parish of Grouville. They lie south west of the island between Jersey and the French coast. Maîtresse Ile has the remains of a Customs House but Les Maisons has no buildings left to be seen. These islands were once quarried during the last century and produced fine sources of famous Jersey granite. When mining ceased to be profitable, activity on the islands became dormant until the First World War when German Forces stationed anti aircraft guns on the islands.

Paternosters

Otherwise referred to as 'Pierres de Lecq' these rocky islets lie north of Jersey and are so called because whenever a ship passes by them sailors are said to have recited the Lord's Prayer. This site was a danger spot for passing craft for hundreds of years and a major disaster occurred in the 16th century when a ship was wrecked and passengers and their children were drowned and the cargo was lost.

The Casquets

These rocks lie north west of Alderney and were a constant threat to Channel vessels for centuries until the first lighthouse was built 250 years ago. The Hougez family lived on them during the last century living in a small cottage and growing their own vegetables. Today a modern lighthouse has replaced the old which is now visible for a radius of 17 miles.

Jethou Island

Jethou lies close by to Herm Island and is Crown property. Sir Charles Hayward is the private tenant and the island is not open to the public. It consists of nearly 100 acres and is a mixture of woodland and scrubland. In the days of piracy, offenders were known to have been strung up on the arms of the trees in 'Fairy Wood' on the north side of the island. Both Herm Island and Jethou provided the setting for 'Fairy Gold' written by the novelist Compton Mackenzie who leased the island in 1920.

Lihou Island

Lihou lies off the west coast of Guernsey and is approachable via a causeway at low tide. It consists of about 18 acres of land and is clearly visible from the mainland. In 1156 a priory was founded by the monks from the Abbey of Mont St Michel. Locals were always suspicious of the goings-on on this little island and a murder of a monk was reported in 1302 committed by the prior's servant. However as time went by the monastery was gradually disbanded and buildings fell into a state of disrepair.

During the last century this area was a centre for 'vraic' gathering and locals from Guernsey had the right to scour the district for agricultural manure and were also allowed to fish. Today the island is let to Col. Patrick Wooton. At one time summer camp was held on the island called the Lihou Youth Fellowship.

Brechou

The island of Brechou faces the north west coast of Sark opposite Gouliot caves. It is occupied by a tenant and few visitors are permitted to land there. According to local lore Brechou is honeycombed with caves made by the descendants of rats which infested the island after deserting a ship doomed with Bubonic plague which sank off the island in 1665.

Flora and Fauna

Herbs, Wild Flowers and their Creative Uses

The Channel Islands are famous for their rich variety of flora. Many of the species to be found can also be seen in Britain. The most interesting varieties, such as exotic palms, have been introduced and these thrive on the mild climate which is marginally warmer than on the mainland. Many of the wild flowers are common to Brittany and some originate from the Mediterranean basin.

The following is a list of plants which may be classed as common to the islands, but which have a surprising number of additional uses.

PROSTRATE GLASS WORT (*Salicornia Ramosissima*)
This is best described as a low lying fleshy green and brown succulent plant. There are nine varieties to be found in Britain, mostly growing in salt marshes and in the Channel Islands you can hunt them out on your wanderings near beaches. They flower between August and September. If you are a glass maker or interested in setting up your own factory you may be interested to know that

252

the soda ash which is produced from burning this plant was a vital ingredient for glass-making in the old days. Cooks will be interested to learn that the annual variety is delectable when eaten as a vegetable, which is common knowledge to people living on the East Coast of England, who have been doing this for years.

DANISH SCURVY GRASS *(Cochlearia Danica)*
If you squint carefully and allow your eyes to travel along stone walls, they may suddenly come to rest on a dwarfed little plant which belongs to the ivy leafed family. It is under 5″ high and has white or pink flowers. This plant thrives in sandy areas and can take root in nooks and crannies of stone walls. This is the plant for anybody who needs a dose of Vitamin C. Ancient mariners relied on it when their supplies ran out after a long voyage before the invention of the vitamin pill.

SEA SPURGE *(Euphorbia Paralias)*
The description of this plant is plump, upright, fleshy and treelike. It looks very succulent and can be found by the coast which is useful to any budding fisherman. If you are passing by with your rod and tackle, you may decide to use the milky juice of the leaves to add to your ground bait as a poison for the fish.

WILD LEEK *(Allum Ampeloprasum)*
When you are staying in Guernsey or on the little island of Herm, this plant will add a pungent addition to any salad dish. Identified by long thin stalks capped with spherical clusters of white or purplish flowers.

FENNEL *(Foeniculum Vulgare)*
This plant can stand up to 4 feet tall and can be found from flowers from late summer to autumn with bright

yellow flowers. The leaves are the most practical items for you to use as garnish for any fish dishes you may be cooking – especially if you happen to bring home some freshly caught mackeral.

HARES TAIL GRASS *(Lagurus Ovatus)*
This attractive grass originates from the Mediterranean and is identified by its round fluffy white heads. When they are dried, the stalks make good additions to any ornamental grass or dried flower arrangement.

LADY'S BEDSTRAW *(Gallum Verum)*
You can find this brilliant yellow plant growing among coastal sands in the islands between July and August. Traditionally the fragant scent made this plant an essential additive to new mown hay used to make up bedding when the islanders slept on mattresses which they made themselves. Campers among you take heed! Another property it has is that it can be used by dairy enthusiasts to curdle the milk for making cheese – it has properties similar to rennet.

REST HARROW *(Onionis Repens)*
This is to be found by the coast too if you can spot the dark pink and white flowers or smell the resinous scent. The roots can be used as a liquorice substitute if you suddenly feel a craving. Incidentally this was a common use in England and in the Channel Islands before the invention of sweets in packets.

TREE MALLOW *(Lavatara Arborea)*
This is a hardy biennial which flowers in summer and can be spotted by its pinkish purple bell shaped flowers. The boiled seeds produce a 'muclilage' similar to the spongy marshmallow.

ROCK SAPPHIRE *(Crithmum Maritimum)*

This is known on the islands as "Perche Pierre" and named after St Peter who is the patron saint of fishermen. It grows near the sea where you can see the light yellow clusters of flowers among the rock crevices. When you find them remember to bring a jar of vinegar with you. The leaves are excellent to eat, bottled and pickled.

ALEXANDERS *(Smyrnium Olusatrum)*

This plant blossoms in spring in coastal areas and by road-sides. You can distinguish it by the strong stalks crowned with clusters of yellow leaves. It originates from Southern Europe where the whole plant has been used in a variety of ways to produce succulent dishes since Ancient times. This is what you do: either cut the stalks and eat as you would celery or boil the leaves and serve as a vegetable. Finally if neither of these appeal the black seeds can be used as a flavouring agent for meat or soups.

RAGWORT

Finally beware of this plant. It flowers from June until late autumn and can be found on wasteground or fields and sometimes embedded in sand-dunes. It is poisonous and dangerous to livestock.

The many wild herbs that thrive in the Channel Islands have been used for centuries to cure a variety of complaints. The current vogue for a natural approach to health has encouraged a rivival of many of the old recipes mentioned below.

VERVAIN

This is a herb known to the islanders as 'herb of grace' and was used as a potent cure for many different ills. It was known to the Druids as a holy herb and was also used by sufferers of 'Scrofula' who sought to be touched by the King when he conducted the ceremony known as Kings Evil. The instructions were clear: the root was dug up carefully so that nothing remained of the plant underground. One half was tied around the neck of the sufferer and the other half was burnt. Finally the leaves of the plant were hung in the chimney to dry out and the illness was said to disappear.

COMFREY *(Console)*
The roots of this plant were said to be effective if the root was mashed and applied carefuly to cuts and bruises.

RUE
This plant was attributed with properties of restoring second sight.

NETTLES
The leaves of the nettle were well known as a cure for cleansing the blood. When boiled and made into nettle tea or 'thé d'orti'.

LEAVED SAGE
The boiled leaves of this plant produced another form of tea said to be an excellent cure for heartburn.

EUPHRASY
This plant was also known as 'eyebright'. It was taken to improve eyesight and make them shiny and attractive.

EARTHWORMS AND OLIVE OIL
In the 17th century this revolting little recipe was taken as a cure for nervous diseases. Live earthworms were boiled to death in oil and kept in a small jar. The ointement was then applied frequently to the affected area!

Channel Island Calendar

Whatever time of year you arrive in the Channel Islands, there is always something going on which relates back to the distant past. The following times of the year have a special significance which are each celebrated in a slightly unusual fashion.

JANUARY 6
Battle of Jersey. This was a decisive victory for the Channel Islands in 1781. It put an end to any further threat of invasion from France during the Napoleonic Wars.

JANUARY 15
Chief Pleas of the Royal Courts.

EASTER
Children used to go round houses in the Channel Island begging for eggs at Eastertime. This tradition originated in Europe where giving gifts at Easter had developed into a customary practice.

EASTER MONDAY
In Jersey a crual sport called 'La Jouote' which consisted of stoning scrawny hens was common practice until it was

prohibited in 1896. The dead bird was claimed as a prize. Today more harmless sport is cycling round the island on a massive pub crawl.

FIRST SUNDAY IN LENT

'La Dimanche des Brandons' is an ancient name for this public occasion which has a similar title in some parts of France. Another name was 'Le jour de Vitres' literally meaning 'Day of Masks'. The origin of the festival was possibly Bacchanalian, when young people on the island made bonfires and celebrated whilst dancing and singing around them.

GOOD FRIDAY

In Jersey and Guernsey hot cross buns are still traditional. However past practices used to include having picnics on the beach and gathering limpets which were cooked and eaten in great quantities. On Sark the local boys used the occasion to proudly sail their prized home made toy boats.

APRIL FOOLS DAY

What happens on that day is never likely to change, but one of the practical jokes in the Channel Islands carried out by island children was to attach rags and shreds of clothing to the coats of passers by.

FIRST SUNDAY IN MAY

Known as 'Milk a Punch Sunday' and still celebrated in Alderney where most island pubs will give free hand outs of this delicious drink made of rum, milk and eggs. In the old days young men and women were entitled to milk whatever cow they could find and beg, borrow or steal eggs from their hens to concoct this traditional brew.

MAY 9
Liberation Day. A public holiday in Jersey, Guernsey and
Sark. In Sark decorated carriages are paraded through the
streets.

MAY 29
The restoration of Charles II is still remembered by school
children. Oak leaves are worn on clothing until 12 noon
and anyone not wearing them is open to pinching and
punching. On the other hand, anyone still wearing leaves
after 12 noon is punched as well so watch out on the 29th.

MIDSUMMER DAY
Midsummer has alway been celebrated throughout history
as a major feast and many pagan rituals arose as a result.
Horns were blown on the islands before June 24th. On
Jersey this was originally the time of year when rents were
due to be paid on the farmland. In Sark, the horses were
garlanded and Midsummer Day was treated as quite a
festival. In Jersey another custom was for parishioners in
St John to row around a rock in the middle of Bonne Nuit
Bay known as 'Le Cheval Guillaum'. This practice was
widely believed to avert ill-luck.

FIRST WEEK OF AUGUST
Alderney Week. General merry making and egg and spoon
races.

LAST THURSDAY IN JULY
Still celebrated in Jersey and Guernsey as the Battle of
Flowers. Also celebrates the coronation of Edward VII.

NOVEMBER 5
Guy Fawkes and bonfire night.

CHRISTMAS DAY

It was a tradition in Guernsey on Christmas Day to bake a milk cake called a 'Gâche dé Détrempée'. A present of these cakes was often sent by a mother to any children on the island who had moved away from home and could not be with their parents to celebrate.

Customs

The Channel Islanders are well known for their independence of character and sturdy outlook. These qualities have developed over the centuries as the result of a hard battle of survival. As an isolated group of islands they had to defend themselves against war and provide themselves with an income, both of which they did successfully.

The islands which were overrun by the Vikings in the 10th century were steeped in superstition and many of the customs which survived on the islands were derived from paganism. Later these were 'glazed over' slightly with Christian ritual, or the times of year that had been celebrated as life giving from time immemorial were conveniently adapted and slotted into the new church calendar. Many of the old customs and traditions in the Channel Islands are no longer in practice. This may be due to the influx of new blood on the islands, or just another sign of progress. The fact that the islands are so small has probably protected them from completely losing many of customs that were lost long before in Europe; but only a few are still preserved today.

LE GRAND MERE DU CHIMQUIERE An upright standing stone which stands in Guernsey in St Martin's Churchyard. It is between 2,500 and 3,000 years old, and there are many myths surrounding it, but no one can offer any concrete explanation as to who put it there. A feature of the stone is that it has recognisable human features which is unusual for such an ancient monument. The people of Guernsey have always regarded it with great reverence, and until comparatively recently offerings of flowers or fruit were to be found at the foot of the stone in the early morning.

THE CLAMEUR DE HARO Even though the administration of the islands has been through many changes many of the names and ancient laws relate back to their Norman origin. The Clameur de Haro for instance is an ancient law relating to property which was instituted by Rollo, one of the first Dukes of Normandy. If these lines were recited in the presence of a witness they had the power to prevent your opponent from carrying out whatever he was doing until the case had been heard in court.

'Haro! Haro! Haro! a l'aide mon Prince. On me fait tort.'
'Haro! Haro! Haro! Help me my Prince, I am being wronged.'

If raised in the right circumstances and the accused was found guilty, he had to pay a fine imposed by the court and stop committing the offence. If wrongly accused, the prosecuting individual was liable to pay the fine for improperly raising the alarm. This procedure is still in use on the island today.

ASSIZE D'HERITAGE Most of the Seigneurial rights are no longer in use on the islands today such as the duties that tenants had to perform. These ranged from cutting the Seigneurs hay and carting wood to cleaning out the pigeon house! One tradition which does survive is the Assize d'Heritage. This occurs at certain times of year when the Seigneurs of some island fiefs attend the Court and answer when the name of their fief is called; an ancient custom which symbolises loyalty to the Sovereign. Another traditional Seigneurial Right was cursed many a time by unhappy tenants on island property. If a man died without offspring and his property was inherited by a nephew or a niece then the Seigneur was entitled to income from the bequeathed estate for a year and a day after the tenant's death – which sometimes amounted to a sizeable sum. This outrageous custom was finally stopped in 1966.

CHEVAUCHEE DE ST MICHEL Another tradition in Guernsey performed by officials on the island was the 'Chevauchée de St Michel'. This was regularly performed every 3 years on the island and was originally intended as an inspection of the public highways. It occurred at mid-summer and was originally practised in the Fief of St Michel performed by the Seigneur and members of this Court. Later this ceremony was adopted by the Parish and became incorporated into the procession at Corpus Christi and was conducted with great ceremony. The last Chevachée which took place in Guernsey was on May 31st 1837.

KING'S EVIL One of the most strange practices in the Channel Islands was known as the 'Kings Evil' (see Herbs, Wild Flowers and their Creative Uses). This was a ceremony which could only be performed by a reigning monarch who 'received' this gift when he was annointed at his coronation. The 'Royal Touch' as it became known, was widely believed to possess healing power particularly in cases of epilepsy, cramp and 'scrofula' which was a form of tuberculosis. This practice was widely used in Guernsey particularly during the reign of Charles II who was said to have extraordinary good powers of healing and touched 92,000 people between 1660 and 1682. In order to stop an onslaught of hypochondriacs, a certificate of authority had to be obtained from a local physician or an authority in the parish to verify that the individual concerned was generally suffering from some complaint! Often people from Guernsey travelled as far as London to be touched in Court. This ceremony continued until the reign of Queen Ann, after which time the islanders had to resort to white witches.

CHEVAUCHÉE L'ANE One practical problem to solving the differences between married couples in the Channel Islands in the Middle Ages was known as 'Chevauchée L'Ane. The couple who were known to quarrel attracted a crowd of islanders every Friday night who hooted and blew through conch shells and horns to drown the noise they made. If quarelling continued, the offenders were often tied back to back and paraded through the town streets on the back of a donkey.

WITCH HUNTING One site in Guernsey which was known to be a meeting place for witches was the island of Lihou on the west coast. A priory was established there in the Middle Ages dedicated to the Virgin Mary and as the site was previously known as a site for witch covens it was no surprise to the natives to learn that the monks were said to practise black magic. When the widespread persecution of witches began in the 15th century, Guernsey was a marked centre for the hunting and condemnation of anybody associated with the black arts. The superstitious fervour which spread through Europe resulted in a large number of trials, particularly between 1560-1640 when 44 people were burnt at the stake and 35 were banished from the island for life.

One legend connected with Lihou Priory concerns a monk who is said to have practised black magic there. One day while returning to the priory and travelling along the causeway, he had entrusted his magic book, containing all his spells, to his servant with strict instruction never to look inside. Lagging behind a little, the young servant suddenly had an irresistable urge to open the book and began reading aloud some of the lines which he found there. Greatly absorbed in this he sat down on the rock nearby quite oblivious of the fact that while he was talking the tide was rising rapidly. His master, caught in the middle of the water saw what was happening and shouted out in despair 'If you cannot read forwards, at least read backwards' but his voice was lost in the sinking waves. A little later the manservant looked up and to his horror discovered that the incantation he had been reading was a spell which had caused the tides to rise and drown the wicked monk who had at last been caught unawares by the black arts that he practised on others.

KNITTING Knitting is a lucrative industry in the Channel Islands. This unusual home industry supplied many Royal Households with Guernsey stockings, and some delightful customs evolved. Knitting reached such a pitch at one stage, that women even knitted on the way to market! In the evening, families and friends met in each other's homes to tell stories and legends, sing and of course, knit. These meetings were known as 'Vielles' and the customs of the islands were perpetuated at these gatherings.

VRAICING The custom of sea-weed gathering was a seasonal one, particularly in Guernsey where the principal seasons were June, July and August. The practice originated in the

Middle Ages and many rights existed for the islanders to collect the vraic from the island shores. When gathered the ashes were dried and then burnt to be used as a rich form of natural fertiliser. A law passed by the Royal Commission in 1607 drew a distinction between 'Vraic scie' which was seaweed cut by hand with a sickle and 'vraic venant' which was drift weed floating free of the rocks. Vraic could be gathered at certain times of the year only and during this season, it was piled high into panniers and led away by horse and cart to be burnt to hot ash. At Midsummer, vraic gathering was treated as a festival. Work was carried out speedily between the tides, and horses and carts were decorated with flowers.

ORMERING 'The 'Ormer' or 'Oreilles des Mers' are a local delicacy in the Channel Islands. It is a flat shell fish that used to be easily found in the 19th century but is scarce today. Ormers originated from the Mediterranean. The nearest description to describe a cooked ormer is like a tender piece of veal, once it has been specially prepared with the traditional recipe which involves a very tasty brown sauce.

Biblography

The Bailiwick of Guernsey by C P Le Huray
The Bailiwick of Jersey by G R Balleine
History of the Channel Islands by Raoul Lempriere
Portrait of the Channel Islands by Raoul Lempriere
Guernsey by G W S Robinson
Jersey by Ward Rutherford
A Short History of Jersey by Joan Stephens (Societe Jersiase)
The German Occupation of the Channel Islands by Charles Cruickshank
The Fief of Sark by A H Ewan & A R de Carteret
Sark my island home by Heather L Baker
Folklore of Guernsey by Marie de Garis
Jersey Folklore by J H L'Amy
Guernsey Folklore by MacCulloch
Access in Jersey A guide for the disabled and for those who have problems getting around. Premier Printers.
The Channel Islands by Wilfred D. Hooke